Maharshi Dayanand Saraswati Book Series- 17

The Science of Śrauta-yajñas

Prof. Ravi Prakash Arya

Chair Professor
Maharshi Dayanand Saraswati Chair (UGC)
Maharshi Dayanand University, Rohtak

AMAZON BOOKS, USA

In association with

INDIAN FOUNDATION FOR VEDIC SCIENCE

1051, Sector-1, Rohtak-124001, Haryana, India
Ph. 09313033917; 9650183260
Email:vedicscience@rediffmail.com; vedicscience@gmail.com
website: https://vedic-sciences.com

First Edition

Christian Era: 2022
Vikram Era: 2079
Kali Era: 5124
Kalpa Era: 1972949124
Brahma Era: 155521972949124

Price: Rs. 250.00

ISBN No. 978-93-94724-09-9

@ Author

Printed by
Indian Foundation for Vedic Science, 1051, Sector-1, Rohtak-124001, Haryana

Contents

Introduction

The Yajña is a key concept of Vedic culture and philosophy. It has been described as the noblest and most excellent act of the Almighty.

यज्ञो वै श्रेष्ठतमं कर्म ।

yajño vai sreṣṭhtamaṁ karma.

There are many types of yajñas. Śrauta yajña, Gṛhya yajña, Pañchamahāyañja, etc. etc. Here the term Śrauta yajña is of great interest for us. The concept of Śrauta yajña can be understood only in the context of Vedas and allied literature. As the present author has pointed out on many occasions, the Vedas are the science of creation, which takes place at three parallel levels, i.e. metaphysical, astrophysical and physical levels in the universe. The Śrauta yajña denotes nothing but the process of this creation. Nothing can be noblest and most excellent work than this act of creation.

Etymologically, the term yajña is formed from the root √yaj, meaning devapujā, saṁgatikaraṇa, and dāna. Devapujā is nothing but comprehending this divine process of creation by symbolically representing it in a fire altar. The actual process of creation takes place because Agni (fire) burns in the Somiki Vedī or fire altar. It is often described that everything in the universe is made up of agni (-ve) and soma (+ve).

अग्निसोमात्मकम् इदं सर्वम् ।

agnisomātmakam idaṁ sarvam

Whenever agni (energy) is ignited in the fire altar of bhūtākāśa, creation takes place. This fact can be easily understood in the context of creation on the Earth. We see that for the creation to occur on Earth, the presence of Sun-rays is essential. Thus, a Śrauta yajña symbolically represents the creation process in the universe and on the Earth. The fire-altar (vedī) represents the Earth so far as the creation on the Earth is concerned and the whole bhūtākāśa (observable space) so far as the creation of the universe is concerned. The Brāhmaṇakāra clearly states that the Earth or Dyau (Bhūtākaśa) space is the fire-altar- इयं पृथिवि वै वेदी (*iyaṁ pṛthivi vai vedī*). The earth/observable space has the same parameters as that of the vedī - यावती वेदी तावती वै पृथिवि (*yāvatī vedī tāvatī vai pṛthivi*). The cosmic yajña (the process of creation on the Earth) takes place with Earth acting as the Vedī and the radiation heating from the Sun playing the role of fire burning in the fire altar of the Earth. It is only due to the sun's rays falling on the earth that the creation takes place. Had there been no radiation heating from the sun, life would not have emerged on the Earth. Similarly, in the context of the origin of the universe, the bhūtākāśa (observable space) with active energy acts as the Somikī Vedī and the active energy acts as fire. That is why it is said that the entire creation is due to a combination of agni and soma. Agni is the -ve charge and soma is a +ve or neutral charge. On the other hand, charged matter particles are described as devas and anti-matter particles as asuras. Devāsura Saṅgrāma (war between devas and asuras) is nothing but the annihilation process of charged particles and their anti-particles. As a result, due to access of charged particles over antiparticles, this creation takes place. So yajña is nothing but the creation of the universe. This, in fact, is the nature of the adhidaivika yajña. In adhidaivika yajña or the process of creation of the universe, bhūtākāśa acts as fire-altar and transformation of activated energy as an oblation. In the process of creation on Earth, the Sun becomes agni and the Earth the vedī.

Similarly, the ādhyātmika yajña (the process of creation at a metaphysical level) is accomplished with the mother acting as the vedī and the father as agni burning in the vedī, the mother. That is why the seer says:

योषा वै वेदी।

yoṣā vai vedī

The further ādhyātmika process of creation is accomplished with Jaṭharāgni acting as the agni and jaṭhara as somīki vedī. The ādhyātmika yajña also takes place in the process of imparting knowledge. In this process, Āchārya or teacher acts as Agni and students as somīki vedī or soma, and imparting of knowledge acts as an oblation. Thus, the Śrauta yajña is the representative of the various processes of creation, with a fire-altar representing the various forms of vedīs called as soma and the fire burning on the altar representing the various forms of agnis involved in various processes of creation. Oblations represent the āhutis offered in metaphysical, cosmic and physical processes of creation.

On the other hand, Vedic scholiasts developed this system of yajña to explain and elucidate the various aspect of spiritual, astronomical and physical sciences. The Sāṅkhāyana Gṛhyasūtra (1.2.18.19) had it as

अधिदैवत् अथाध्यात्म अधियज्ञमिति त्रयम्।
मन्त्रेषु ब्राह्मणेषु चैव श्रुतमित्य्-अभिधीयते।।

adhidaivat athādhyātma adhiyajñamiti trayam.
mantreṣu brāhmaṇeṣu caiva śrutamity-abhidhīyate.

A close perusal of Brāhmaṇas confirms this fact. For instance, Ś.Br. 10.2.5.1&2 relates the aim of agnicayana ceremony to ātmasanskāra or self-purification as,

तथैवैतद् यजमानः एथाः पुरः प्रपद्याभयेऽनाष्ट्रा एतम् आत्मानम् संस्कुरुते ।

*tathaivaitad   yajamānaḥ   ethāḥ   puraḥ
prapadyābhaye'nāṣṭrā etam ātmānam saṁskurute.*

We may refer here Sāyaṇa's commentary:

तथाऽयम् यजमानोऽपि उपसदोर् मध्ये अग्निचयनेन् आत्मानम् संस्कुरुते ।

*tathā'yam yajamāno'pi upasador madhye agnicayanen
ātmānam saṁskurute.*

At another place the *Ś.Br.* (10.2.3.15) describes all the Yajñas aiming at *ātma-saṁpādana* or self-accomplishment, e.g. *sarvair hi yajñair ātmānaṁ saṁpannaṁ vide*

At yet another place, Ś.Br. (11.5.3.1) proclaims agnihotra as the expounder of Ātman or Brahman, i.e. supreme self, e.g.

शौचेयो ह प्राचिनयोग्य उद्दालकम् आरुणिम् आजगाम ब्रह्मोद्यम् अग्निहोर्तं विविदिसिष्यामि इति ।

Śauceyo ha prācinayogya uddālakam āruṇim ājagāma brahmodyam agnihortaṁ vividisiṣyāmi iti.

We come across such references in the Ś.Br. as describe the two-fold objects of Darśpūrṇamāsa and Chāturmāsya sacrifices, viz., Ātmayājītva and Devayājītva, i.e. spiritual as well as astronomical one. For example, Sāyaṇa's commentary at 11.5.2.1 is noteworthy. According to him, as we have shown the spiritual as well as the astronomical purpose of Darśa-pūrṇamāsa yāgas, similarly to illustrate the two-fold purpose of Chāturmāsya yāga, we state here a legend to associate the various limbs of the body with the various parts of yajña.

यथा दर्श पूर्णमास याजिनः आत्मयाजिल्वं चेति द्वैविध्यं दर्शितम् एवं चातुर्मास्य याजिनोऽपि तथाल्वं दर्शयितुं शरिरावयव कल्पनं आख्यिकया रचयति ।

yathā darsa pūrṇamāsa   yājinaḥ ātmayājitvaṁ ceti

dvaividhyaṁ darśitam evaṁ cāturmāsya yājino'pi tathātvaṁ darśyituṁ śarīrāvayava kalpanaṁ ākhyikayā racayati.

In addition to the above, the yajñas were also performed in a time-bound manner starting from one day to a thousand years to retain the astronomical records of various movements of the Earth, Moon and various other planets and stars. For instance, *ekāhahin yāga* represented the earth's rotation on its axis. The year-long satra in the *Aitreya Brāhmaṇa* (Book III & IV) represented the phenomenon of the Earth's revolution around the Sun. Martin Hauge writes in his introduction to the *Aitareya Āraṇyaka* (P.48) 'The satras lasted for one year were nothing but an imitation of the Sun's yearly course. They were divided into two distinct parts, six months of 30 days each. In the midst of both was the viṣuvan, i.e., the equator or the central day cutting the whole satra into two halves (Uttarāyaṇa and Dakṣiṇāyana).' Some yāgas were also carried out to celebrate the reconciliation of various years; for example, according to Nidāna Sūtra (10.5), five-day yāga was done at the end of each civil year of 360 days to reconcile the civil year to the solar year of 365 days. Similarly, the reconciliation of the synodic lunar year of 354 days was done to the solar year of 365 1/4 days through ekādaśa rātra ahīnayāga performed at the end of each synodic year. For the reconciliation of the civil year of 360 days to the solar year of 365.25 days, Atirātra yāgas of 4, 5, or 6 days were also performed at the end of the civil year. The *Taittirīya Saṁhitā* (1.1.8) mentions a controversy about the number of days on which Atirātra yāgas were to be performed. It says the four atirātras make the year incomplete, while six atirātras give excess. So, five atirātras are the best for attaining unison with seasons.

Similarly, 12 years" satra in Naimiṣa forest described in the *Tāṇḍya Brāhmaṇa* (25.6. 4) represents the Bṛhaspati or Jupiter's course around the Sun in twelve years.

In the *Taittirīya Saṅhitā* (*TS.*) (12th chapter), there is a mention of Sāyana sattra named Vaiśvasṛja yāga, symbolizing the entire life span of the present creation of this Kalpa. This Kalpa has a total life span of 1000 mahāyugas, calculated as 4,32,00,00,000 years.

In the *TS.* (3rd Kāṇḍa) we find details about Nakṣatreṣṭi wherein separate puronuvākyā and yājyā mantras are given for each Nakṣatra. There the 14 Deva-nakṣatras beginning with Kṛttikās and 14 Yama Nakṣatras beginning with Anurādhā are referred to in Anuvāka two.

Thus, the physical Yajñas were performed in precise conformity with the cosmic yajñas going on in the universe or the Brahma Yajña going on at the spiritual level. Little mistakes in the performance of physical yajñas could amount to serious threats to understanding the natural course. Hence, every bit of accuracy was maintained at all costs. To avoid such mistakes, separate chapters were devoted to the subject of Yajña-chhidra (flaws in the performance of yajña).

In addition, Yajña was also developed as a tāntrika technology in the form of Devayajña to materialize various astronomical phenomena like rainmaking and anti-rain. For instance, the Agniṣomīya Paśuyāga was not the sacrifice in which animals were used to be killed. Rather, it had a twofold significance. At the ādhyātmika level, it signified the charging of consciousness with knowledge; at the astronomical level, it signified an operation for rainmaking.

In this monograph, we shall try to explain the scientific import of some of the important Śrauta yajñas and fire-altars.

Prof. Dr. Ravi Prakash Arya
Maharshi Dayanand Saraswati Chair (UGC)
Maharshi Dayanand University, Rohtak
vedicscience@gmail.com
Ph. 9313033917; 9650183260

Science of Vedic Fire-altars

The system of Yajña was developed in Vedic times to explain and elucidate the various aspects of spiritual, astronomical and terrestrial sciences. Not only did Yajñas point to the various terrestrial, spiritual and astronomical phenomena, but the fire-altars, too, that were constructed to perform the figurative and symbolical Yajñas also symbolised by their area, shape and construction material the various aspects of terrestrial, astronomical and spiritual sciences.

For instance, altars were used to educate people on the shape and movements of stars and planets. In Taittirīya Saṁhitā (7.4.10), a question has been raised regarding the centre and the farthest end of the earth.

पृच्छामि त्वा परमन्तः पृथिव्याः, पृच्छामि त्वद् भुवनस्य नाभिम् ।

pṛcchāmi tvā paramantaḥ pṛthivyāḥ, pṛcchami tvad bhuvanasya nābhim.

'I ask you the farthest end of the earth and the centre of it.'

The answer given in a simple manner by way of an altar was:

वेदिमाहुः परमन्तः पृथिव्याः ।

vedimāhuḥ paramantaḥ pṛthivyāḥ.

'The altar is the farthest end of the earth and the centre of it.

Now, we shall examine the various features of altars in terms of shape, area, and construction material and try to answer their various significances.

Yūpa

Fire altars were always furnished with a Yajñīya stake or Yūpa. Oblation material was used to be stored at the site of Yūpa. Yūpa was a gnomon, which gave Yajamāna an accurate estimate of various timings and seasons. Kutub Minar in Delhi and the Minar-e-Jam in Gandhar are examples of Vedha-yūpas (observatories) constructed by Varāhamihira at Mihiravali (Modern Meharuli) and Gandhar, respectively. They were called as Vaidha yūpa yāna. The northern door of this Vedha-yūpa (observatory) or Kutub Minar was for observing the Pole star and was surrounded by 27 temples, each representing one of the 27 constellations. Thus, it was installed as an observatory to record the time. Later, it was converted into a Minaret by a Muslim ruler, Kutubudin-Aibak. All 27 temples were demolished by him. Kutub, in Arabic, means pole star. Thus, Kutub Minar was nothing else but a representation of ancient Vedic Yūpa. There was also a tradition of performing various Yajñas according to various seasons. The seers identified that in the twilight of various seasons, just as at dawn and twilight of day and night, the occurrence of viruses takes place. To control such viruses occurring due to the change of weather, herbal Yajñas (Bhaiṣajya Yajñas) were performed with a particular type of oblation material mainly selected for the purpose.

ऋतुसन्धिषु हि व्याधिर्जायते ।

ṛtusandhiṣu hi vyādhirjāyate[1]

---

[1] *Kauṣitaki Brāhamaṇa* (5.1)

Since it was with the help of Yūpa that the proclamation of setting in a new season was made possible, the various type of oblation material was stored at the site of Yūpa, so that oblations of proper material required in a proper season could be made because of the prevalent season.

Kind of Bricks to be laid in Fire-alters

The kinds of bricks to be laid in the construction of particular fire altars depended upon the phenomenon symbolised by a particular Yajña to be performed in the fire altar. For instance, in the Vaisvasṛja Yāga mentioned in the *Taittirīya Saṅhitā*, all animate and inanimate, all males, all females and all sex-less beings, all animals, all stones, all rivers, all plants and trees, all metals like iron, copper, silver and gold are to become the bricks of its sacrificial-altar as also all the direction, whole sky and whatever is in it and all spray and snow, all rays, lightening-flashes, all clouds, all waters in wells, streams and seas, light, wind, fire, the sun, the moon, Mitra, Varuṇa, Bhaga, Satya and Śraddhā, all deities, all the stars, all the Ṛks, Yajus, Sāmans, and Atharvāṅgiras as also, Itihāsa, Purāṇa and Sarpadeva Yajañas, all the worlds, days and nights, fortnights, months, etc. everything that has been and will be made the bricks. Since the Vaisvasṛja Yāga represented the present creation, its altar consisted of bricks representing all objects of creation.

Type of alters

A considerable part of Vedic Yajñas deals with altar construction. An altar was, in fact, the representation of the earth, as is obvious from the context of Vedī-karaṇa occurred in the *Taittirīya Saṅhitā* (*TS.*) (1.1.9). There, it has clearly been mentioned that the earth (or other planets) is the altar.

पृथिवी देवयजनि, पृथिव्यै देवयजन्यै ।

pṛthivī devayajani, pṛthivyai devayajanyai

At another place, the *TS.* (2.6.4.) again, confirm this view as:

एतावती वै पृथिवि यावती वेदी ।

etāvatī vai pṛthivi yāvatī vedī

Here, we may also remember that the earth (or the earth like other planets) sustains the physical creation of the universe. That is why the earth or planets are called altar or Vedī. There is a Gārhapatya altār where the fire keeps burning. For doing Yajña, fire is carried from the Gārhapatya altār to the Āhavanīya altar. Gārhapatya altār, in fact, represents the perennial source of energy located in stars in the universe. From the perennial source of energy, the creation is led further on the planets. That is why the fire is carried away from the Gārhapatya altar to the Āhavanīya altar. Gārhapatya altar is also drawn as circular shaped, representing the spherical starry bodies in the universe. Āhavanīya altar represents the further ongoing creation on the planets like Earth. Thus, Āhavanīya altar represents the planetary bodies in the universe. The planet Earth, in its earliest stages, when it was about to sustain its creation on it, assumed the shape of a square. This shape of the earth in the Purāṇas is figuratively called a lotus-petalled shape. (Cf. supra pp. 29-31). The first creation of our solar system took place on the four-petalled lotus-shaped earth. Since this square-shaped earth or four petalled-shaped earth became the basis of the first-ever creation of our universe, the Āhavanīya altar is constructed in a square shape. In fact, the square shape of the main altar or uttarvedī symbolised the (uttara) creation of the planetary bodies in the universe. The circular Gārhapatya altar's alteration into a square-shaped Āhavanīya altar with the area remaining unaltered also solves, on the other hand, the geometric problem of squaring a circle and vice versa. This problem, as we know, is considered among the earliest considered in ancient geometry. See fig.1 below :

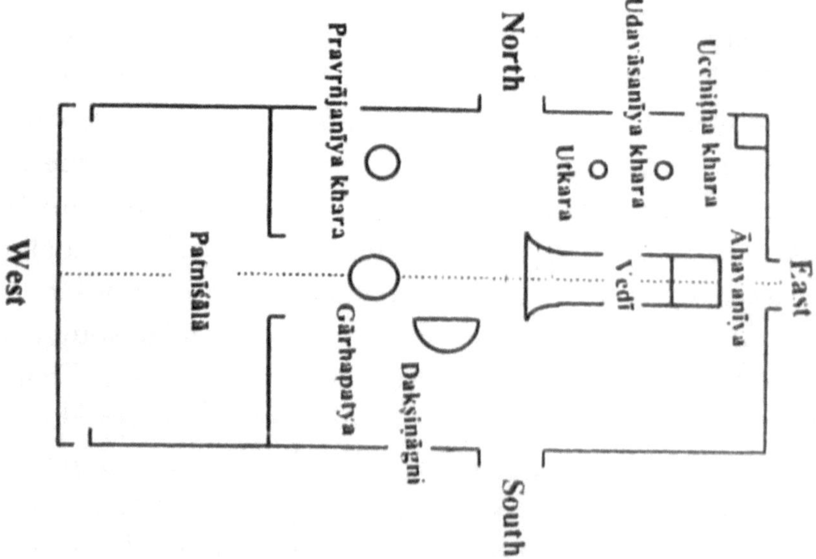

Fig 1 Altar of Darśapūrṇamāsa yāga or Dārśikī Vedī

The Altar of Darśapūrṇamāsa yāga or Dārśikī Vedī is drawn in fig. 1. In the construction of the Dārśikī altar which entirely represents the earth, one more altar is drawn known as the altar of Dakṣiṇāgni or Anvāhāryapachana. Its shape is always like that of a crescent moon, but the area is also equal to that of the circular Gārhapatya altar. This altar symbolised the Soma, i.e. moon, as well as the waters and vegetation that grew on the earth. Whatever grows on the earth or originates from the earth is called Soma. That is why the moon is called Soma- *candramā vai somaḥ* and like-wise vegetations are called Soma- *somo vanaspati*. Grains are also called Soma- *annam vai somaḥ*. Herbs are also called Soma- *somo ausadhiḥ*. Similarly, waters are called Soma. Thus, the anvāhāryapachana altar, which in a physical sense is used for preparing meals to be eaten by Yajamāna (performer of Yajña) or priest, represents the product of the earth. Here, it may also be made clear that the provision of Dakṣiṇā after Yajña represented not the donation to be made to the priest but the fruitful result of the Yajña in the form of new creation. That is why Yajña without Dakṣiṇā was considered as useless. Yajña symbolises the creation; if its purpose is not served, it will be useless. Yajamāna and priests also eat the meals prepared on Dakṣiṇāgani as the fruit of Yajña. Since no particular shape is given to the Dakṣiṇāgni altar representing all the products of the earth. The most appropriate shape to be given to this altar is that of a Crescent moon, the moon being the biggest product of the earth. The Crescent Moon was taken to distinguish this altar from the other two altars.

Instead of the Gārhapatya altar as represented by the Dārśikī vedī, Mahāvedi also consisted of two other types of altars. The first one was called uttarvedī, representing the further creation.

Other six altars representing the six other planets, which influence the bio-life on the earth, were also drawn in a square shape at a particular place of Mahāvedī known as sadomaṇḍap. Sadas is the representative of space. In fact, seven grahas, six planets plus the sun, were discovered by Vedic seers that influenced the biosphere of the earth. This is the reason why the scholars named the days of the week only after these seven planets. These six altars were also drawn as squares since they helped further the earth's creation. Thus, the altar construction was done given the past, present and future creation in the universe, or the other way around, it can be maintained that altars were drawn representing the six planets of the present solar system given their impact on the earth.

Construction of alter:

For the construction of the altar, one has to move from south to north, which is called Udak-krama, and also from west to east, known as prāk-karma. As it has already been pointed out that the vedī or altar symbolised the earth, the directions of the altar drawing or construction also symbolise the polar wanderings of the earth and its rotation. For instance, the west-to-east movement represents the earth's rotation from west to east. The South-to-north movement represents the oscillation of the earth's magnetic pole from south to north pole. In fact, the polar oscillations and rotation of the earth caused the movement of the land mass from south to north and west to cast. This geological phenomenon is popularly known as plate tectonics or continental drift.

It seems that altars were constructed from south to

north and west to east in view of the earth's rotation, polar wanderings, and continental drift.

No. of bricks to be laid in alters:

Fire-altars were surrounded by 360 enclosing stones. Of these, 21 were around the earth altar, 78 around the antarikṣa altar and 261 around the sky altar. In the case of the Dārśikī altar, antarikṣa was meant for the hydrosphere surrounding the lithosphere and the sky was meant for the magnetosphere of the earth surrounding the earth (hydro + lithosphere). In fact, the full circle of the earth, including its atmosphere or, say, total Biosphere, was taken to be 360, of which 21 parts that are 6%, were measured as part of the lithosphere.

If we equalise the 6% part to the actual diameter of the lithosphere, i.e., around 3200 km. The hydrosphere, being 78 parts of 360, works out around 22% of the total sphere and, as such, amounts to be around 9500 km. in diameter. The total diameter of the lithosphere plus hydrosphere (known as earth) comes to around 127000 km. which is the actual diameter of the earth. The magnetosphere, being 261 parts or 72%, extends about another height of about 20000 km. This height has been identified by modern research into Geophysics as the 'Von Alen Radiation belt.' The study of this belt could have become possible after 1958 through satellites under the discipline of Magneto hydrodynamics. This belt saves the earth from solar radiation and has the most negligible influence on the surface of the earth. Thus, it is clear from the foregoing that Vedic scholiasts discovered every bit of the biosphere that is involved in the sustenance of life on the earth.

The various altars were built in five layers of a

thousand bricks of specified shapes. Five layers represent the five fold creation manifesting into Akasa (space), Vayu (air or gas), Agni (fire), Apah (water/liquid matter) and Prthivi (earth or solid matter). The Number thousand was again the symbol of 1000 mahāyugas, the total life span of the bio-life on the earth. Since the altar was the representation of the earth. The 1000 bricks symbolised earth's ability to sustain biolife till 1000 mahāyugas. The *Bhagavadgitā* (8.17), a part of the *Mahābhārata*, also presents the concept of Brahma's day and night consisting of 1000 yugas each.

सहस्रयुगपर्यन्तम् अहर्यद् ब्राह्मणो विदु: ।
रात्रिम् युगसहस्रान्तम् ता तेऽहोरात्रविदो जनाः । ।

sahasrayugaparyantam aharyad brāhmano viduh.
rātrim yugasahasrāntam tā te'horātravido janāh.

Area of fire-alters:

The main altar was an area of 7½ units and this area was taken to be equivalent to the nominal year of 360 days. Thus one unit represented 48 days.

According to a well known altar-ritual, altars should be constructed in a sequence of 95, with progressively increasing area. An increase in area per year was one unit or say 48 tithis required to make a nakṣatra year of 324 tithis equal to the solar year of about 372 tithis. But there is a residual excess which in 95 years adds up to 48 tithis; it appears that after this period a correction was made. The 95 years cycle corresponds to the tropical year being equal to 365.24675 days. The cycles needed to harmonise various motions led to the concept of increasing periods and world ages.

Shapes of alters:

As stated earlier, fire-altar represented the earth. The *TS.* (2.6.4) has clearly substantiated this view. It is stated therein :

एतावती वै पृथिवि यावति वेदी: ।

etāvatī vai pṛthivi yāvati vedīḥ

The parameter of the altar is equivalent to that of the earth.

Before proceeding further with the various shapes of the altar, it is essential to point out here that the earth has undergone the change of several shapes since the time of its origin. This has also been proved by modern research in Geophysics. According to R.A. Daly, after the formation of the solid crust of the earth and the primaeval scar due to the separation of the mass that became the moon, the globe stood divided into a land hemisphere and a water hemisphere represented by the site of the Pacific. The land hemisphere itself was shaped into two polar caps, two mid-latitude furrows and an equatorial continent. All the continents were roughly gentle domes. See fig. 2 below:

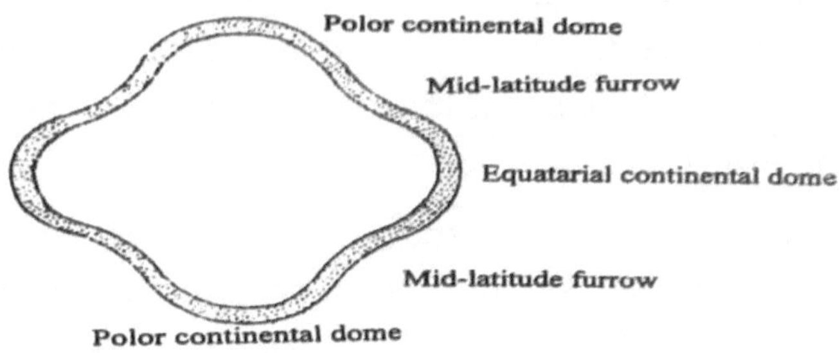

Fig 2 Four-petalled Earth

A similar type of conclusion regarding the earlier shape of the earth was derived by Jeans on the basis of the study of the rotational stability of planetary bodies. According to him, after the origin of the Moon, the earth rotated into the figure of a pear. The protruding parts of the pear were two continents. After it got cooled, the two continents attracted to each other making the equatorial continents out. See fig. 3 below :

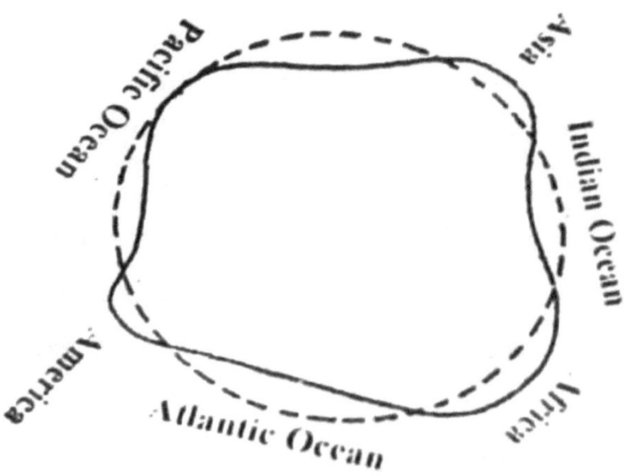

Fig 3 Four-petalled Earth

Thus at the earliest stage, the earth's lithosphere was more like a square. This shape of the earth is figuratively called in the Purāṇas as a four-petalled lotus shape. The first creation took place on the four-petalled lotus-shaped earth. The Vedic scholiasts were already familiar with these facts. hence, they constructed the (Saumikī) Mahāvedī as an isosceles trapezoid having bases of 24 and 30 and a width of 36.

The main altar was also built in five layers with a basic square shape. All this shows that the earliest origin of the earth took place in the shape of four domed squares, which were conceived in Geophysics research.

This fact has been recalled in the Paurāṇika tradition as the four petals of the lotus from which the world was created. The basic square shape was modified to several, such as turtle and falcon. See fig.4 below:

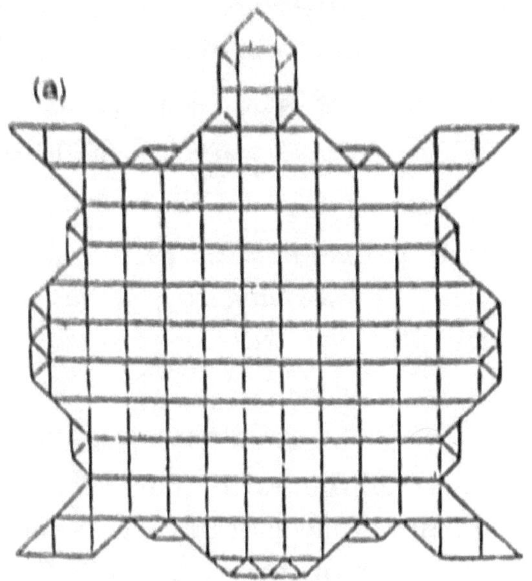

Fig 4 Turtle-shaped altar

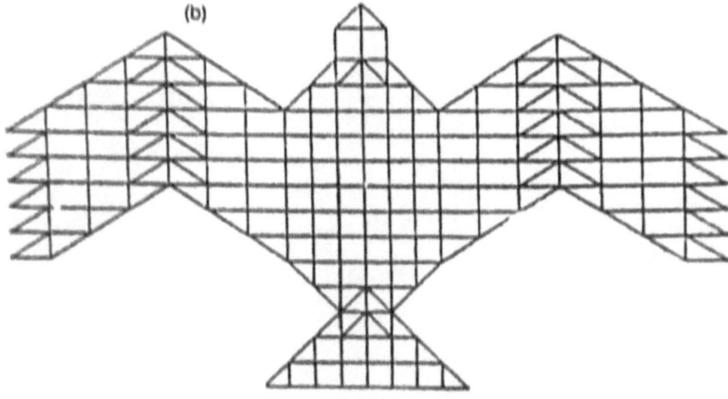

Fig 5 Falcon-shaped altar

After the earth cooled down, it became worthy of creation. After getting cooled, it occupied the shape of a

Turtle. According to Śatapatha Brāhmaṇa (7.5.1.5), Prajāpati created the world by shaping the earth into a turtle-like form. This is why Prajāpati is called a turtle. Kaśyapa, or the part of the Sun, separated as the earth turned turtle. Hence, the world being created on the turtle-formed earth came to be designated as Kaśyapa.

स यत् कुर्मो नाम, एतद्वै रूपम् कृवा प्रजापतिः प्रजा असृजत। यदसृजताकरोत् तदकरोत्। तस्मात् कूर्मः, कश्यपो वै कूर्मस् तस्माद् आहुः सर्वाः काश्यप्या इति।

sa yat kurmo nāma, etadvai rūpam kṛvā prajāpatiḥ prajā asṛjata. yadasṛjatākarot tadakarot.. tasmāt kūrmaḥ, kaśyapo vai kūrmas tasmād āhuḥ sarvāḥ kāśyapyā iti.

Here, the turtle shape of the altar represents the turtle-like portion of the earth that refers to the earth with sialic (hard upper layer of the crust) and the basaltic (lower crystallised part of the crust) layers floating on the mass of moving molten sub-crystal matter. The thermal convection current theories in Geophysics ascertain a similar type of earth's formation. See fig. 5 below:

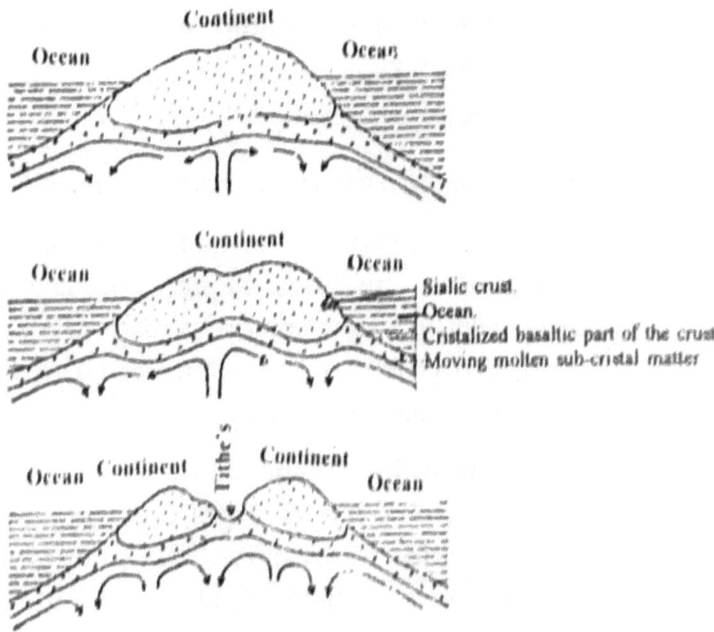

Fig 5 Hard crust of the Earth

Thus it is crystal clear from the foregoing that the turtle shaped fire-alter represented the geophysical aspect of the terrestrial science. Apart from the above facts, here it may also be pointed out that Viṣṇu is the representative of the created world whereas Śiva represents decreation and Brahmā, the creation. The continuation of the creation is symbolised in the Brāhmaṇas as the Yajña or Sṛṣṭi-yajña. That is why, Brāhmaṇakāra's say: *viṣṇur vai yajñaḥ*. Viṣṇu as per Paurāṇika records incarnated in the form of Kūrma or turtle. Viṣṇu's this incarnation in the form of tortoise also pin-points that creation took place after the earth assumed the shape of a turtle.

The another modification of the altar was in the form of a falcon (śyena). In fact, falcon or syena has been described as the form of agni or electricity. The *TS.*

(5.3.11.2) equates apaḥ and śyena and further states that śyena is a form of agni, e.g.

अप्सु सदसि श्येन सदसीत्याहैतद्वा अग्ने रूपम् ।

apsu sadasi śyena sadasītyāhaitadvā agne rūpam

Here the altar's modification into a falcon shape is the pointer to the fact that the physical creation is run by āpaḥ and agni represented by a falcon. This is the reason why, the Paurāṇika mythology has identified the falcon as the vehicle of Viṣṇu (created world).

Altars were also modified to the shape of ratha-chakra or the wheel of a chariot with its navel and spokes. The wheel shaped modification represented the phenomenon of earth's revolution around the Sun. Here the Sun being the navel and elliptic path of the earth being the circle of the wheel and spokes being the 12 zodiac signs or months of the year. In other words, it may be stated that the wheel shaped modification symbolised the Kāla-chakra or the wheel of time. This Kāla-chakra has been described in the *RV*.1.164.2 as under:

द्वादशारम् न हि तज्जराय वर्वर्ति चक्रम् परिद्यामऋतस्य ।

dvādaśāram na hi tajjarāya varvarti cakram paridyāmaṛtasya.

The wheel (of time) having twelve spokes (months) revolved round the heavens, but it doesn't wear out.

In addition to terrestrial and astronomical representations as shown above; fire-altars also had equivalence in Adhyātma, particularly in physiology. A striking example of this is the Dārśikī-vedī i.e. the altar for Darśa-pūrṇamāsa yāga. In fact, Darśa and Pūrṇa-māsa are associated with the moon. Darśa means new moon Pūrṇamāsa means full moon. Darśapūrṇamāsa yāga has a twofold significance, one deva-yājitva, i.e. astronomical, another ātma-yājitva, i.e. physiological or psychological. In the astronomical sense, it refers to the phenomenon of the origin or rising of the moon. In a physiological sense, it symbolises the birth of a child. Darśa represents the old decaying man, and Pūrṇmāsa is the full-blown young man. So far as the origin or rising of the moon is concerned, the earth acts as the altar ground: *etāvati vai pṛthivī yāvati vedī*, and so far as the birth of a child is concerned, a woman is the altar ground- *yoṣā vai vedīr vṛṣā vedaḥ* (*Ś.Br.* 1.9.2.24). In fact, the physiology of a woman is considered to be somīya one and that of a man to be āgneya one. Since Darśa-pūrṇamāsa, in a physiological sense, is related to the birth of a child. It is clearly stated in the *Ś. Br.* as under:

स यो हैव विद्वान् पौर्णमासेन पौर्णमासीं यजते अमावास्येनामावास्याम् क्षिप्र एव पाप्मानं अपहते क्षिप्र प्रजायते। (श.ब्रा ११.१.३.७)

sa yo haiva vidvan paurṇamāsena paurṇamāsīṁ yajate amāvāsyenāmāvāsyām kṣipra eva pāpamānaṁ apahate kṣipra prajāyate. (Ś.Br. 11.1.3.7)

Sayaṇa-bhāṣya is worth noticing on the above observations of the *Śatapatha*. Accordingly-

अल्प एव काले कृत्स्न पापरूपं पुत्रपौत्रादिप्रजा समृद्धिम् च प्राप्नुवन्।

alpa eva kāle kṛtsna pāpa-rūpam pūtra pautrādi prajā smṛddhim ca prāpnuvan.

As such its altar symbolises the physiology of a woman. The process of this yāga goes ahead of the full moonlight to the least moonlight, and the altar is narrow on the front side, wide on the backside and pressed in the middle part, thus symbolising exactly a lady. It has been explained clearly in Āpastamba Śulva Sūtra (4.18.19) as :

परस्तादहीयस्नि पश्चात् प्रथियसी मध्येसन्नततरा एवमिव हि योषास्विति दर्शिवया वेदेर् विज्ञायते ।

parastādahīyasni paścāt prathiyasī madhyesannatatarā evamiva hi yoṣāsviti darśivayā veder vijñāyate.

Similar idea is recorded in the *Taittirīya Brāhmaṇa* (1.2.1.27) as :

चतुः शिखण्डा युवतिः सुपेशा ।

catuḥ sikhaṇḍā yuvatiḥ supeśā

Somayāga also symbolises the creation of the world and the phenomenon of rain formation. This is why Saumikī vedī is also constructed with the same idea in mind. It is also shaped like the physiology of a woman. Similarly, altars represent the physiology of a man, the Yajamāna, and the divine man Prajāpati or Viṣṇu.

Apart from the above-cited equivalence in astronomy and physiology, the altar and its modifications exhibit several ideologies and purposes behind their constructions. For instance, the *S.Br.* (3.1.1.11) while relating the astronomical purpose of the construction of the altar, states that Devas, the scholars who constructed this altar, got their knowledge extended to the heaven or inter-stellar space with the help of this altar, or it elevates the one who performs in it to the level of Astronomer, Deva-hood. Whoever wants to become Deva, well versed in astronomical creation and its knowledge should perform Yajña in this altar.

अतो वै देवा दिवम् उपोदक्रमन् देवान् वा एष उपोक्रामति यो दीक्षते, स देवे

देववजने यजते ।

ato vai devā divam upodakraman devān vā eṣa upotkrāmati yo dīkṣate, sa deve devavajane yajate.

The meaning is clear: Whoever wants to gain knowledge of astronomical creation (divinehood) should perform yajña on the altar. Here, divinehood means excellence in astronomical scientific knowledge. Scholars were always described as devas—vidvānso vai devāḥ. So, to gain scientific knowledge is to become a deva.

Similarly, altar modifications were also made due to specific ideologies or purposes. The following various ideologies, motives or purposes behind modifying the main altar into various shapes have been depicted in Kāmya Citi Prakaraṇa of the *TS.* (5.4.11):

1. Whoever wants to have students and impart knowledge to them should pile Chhandaścit.

छन्दश्चितं चिन्वीत पशुकामः पशवो वै छन्दांसि पशुमानेव भवति ।

chandaścitaṁ cinvīta paśukāmaḥ paśavo vai chandānsi paśumāneva bhavati -(5.4.11.1).

Chhandaściti is an alter for Brahmayajña, or in most modern terms, infrastructure for studies.

2. Whoever wants to receive the treasure of knowledge of space or the celestial sphere, i.e., sunlight, rain, and air, should modify the altar to the shape of a falcon.

श्येनचितिम् चिन्वीत सुवर्गकामः श्येनो वै वयसाम् प्रतिष्ठः श्येन एव भूत्वा सुवर्ग लोकम् पतति ।

Śyenacitim cinvīta suvargakāmaḥ śyeno vai vayasām pratiṣṭhaḥ śyena eva bhūtvā suvargaṁ lokam patati

(5.4.11.2, see also Āp.Śul.Sū. 15.1)

Actually, modifying the main square altar into a falcon shape also solved the geometric problem of dividing a big square into many small rectangles and squares.

3. Whoever wants himself to gain abhyudaya (prosperity and progress) in this world, he should pile a duck shaped altar.

कङ्कचितम् चिन्वीत यः कामयेत शीर्षण्वान् अमुष्मिन्ल्लोके स्यामिति शीर्षन्वानेवामुष्मिन्ल्लोके भवति। (५.४.११.४)

kankacitam cinvīta yaḥ kāmayeta śīrṣaṇvān amuṣminnloke syāmiti sīrṣanvānevāmuṣminnloke bhavati.

(5.4.11.4)

4. Those who want to excel in knowledge of all the directions should modify the altar to resemble an Alaja bird.

अलजचितम् चिन्वीत प्रतिष्ठा कामश्च तिस्रो दिशो दिक्ष्वेव प्रति-तिष्ठति। (५.४.११.४)

alajacitam cinvīta pratiṣṭhā kāmaśca tisro diśo dikṣveva prati-tiṣṭhati. (5.4.11.4)

5. Who wants to abolish impediments on his way of gaining knowledge, he should pile the Prauga-shaped altar, i.e. a triangle-shaped altar. This modification also solved the geometric problem of the conversion of a square into a triangle.

प्रौगचितम् चिन्वीत भ्रातृव्यान् प्रै व भ्रातृव्यान् नुदत।

praugacitam cinvīta bhrātṛvyān prai va bhrātṛvyān nudata.

6. Whoever wants to abolish present and future

impediments on his way of acquiring the knowledge of universe, should pile a Prauga on both sides. Meaning thereby, the piling of a Prauga alter equips a scholar with all necessary tools of acquiring knowledge.

उभयतः प्रौगम् चिन्वीत यः कामयेत प्रजातान् भ्रातृव्यान् नुदेयं प्रति जनिष्यमाणानिति प्रैव जातान् भ्रातृव्यान् नुदते प्रति जनिष्यमाणान्।

ubhayataḥ praugam cinvīta yaḥ kāmayeta prajātān bhrātṛvyān nudeyam prati janiṣyamāṇāniti praiva jātān bhrātṛvyān nudate prati janiṣymāṇān.

In fact, this modification also solves the geometric problem of converting a square into a rhombus.

7. A person who finds it difficult to acquire knowledge should pile the shape of a wheel of a chariot. The wheel of a chariot is the vajra (ignorance-removing tool). Thus, when he piles a wheel, he shoots the enemy of ignorance with vajra.

रथचक्रचितम् चिन्वीत भ्रातृव्यान् वज्रो वै रथो वज्रमेव भ्रातृव्येभ्यः प्रहरति।

rathacakracitam cinvīta bhrātṛvyān vajro vai ratho vajrameva bhrātṛvyebhyaḥ praharati.

8. Who wants to have grains, he should modify the shape of a drona or a circular vessel. Since grain is contained in a vessel shaped alter.

द्रोणचितम् चिन्वीत अन्नकामो द्रोणे वा अन्नं भ्रियते स योन्येवान्नम् अवरुन्धे।

droṇacitam cinvīta annakāmo droṇe vā annam bhriyate sa yonyevānnam avarundhe.

This modification also solved the geometric problem of the circulation of a square.

9. Whoever wants posterity, he should extend the main altar in all directions, samuhya here means

extension in all direction.

समुह्यं चिन्वीत पशुकामः पशुमानेव भवति ।

samuhyaṁ cinvīta paśukāmaḥ paśumāneva bhavati.

This gave the idea of the problem of extending a square in all four directions.

10. Who aspires for the head-ship of a group, he should pile a mound on the altar. Paricâyya means 'mound'.

परिचाय्यम् चिन्वित ग्रामकामो ग्राम्येव भवति ।

paricāyyam cinvita grāmakāmo grāmyeva bhavati.

11. Whoever wants to thrive in old age, he should modify the altar to the shape of a crematorium.

श्मशानचितम् चिन्वीत यः कामयेत पितृलोक ऋध्नुयामिति पितृलोक एवर्ध्नोति ।

śmaśānacitam cinvīta yaḥ kāmayeta pitṛloka ṛdhnuyāmiti pitṛloka evardhnoti.

Agniṣomīya Paśuyāga
An Operation for Rainmaking

Vedas are the first and foremost record of the significant advances made by humanity. Vedic Ṛṣis explored the creation undergoing the journey from metaphysical through physical to astrophysical. These were known as three aspects of creation: ādhyātmika (metaphysical), ādhibhautika (physical) and ādhidaivika (astrophysical). During their explorations, they found that all three aspects are interdependent. Physical is based on the Astrophysical aspect, and Astrophysical on metaphysical, the metaphysical aspect being the primary source of evolution. The other way around, it can be maintained that from the metaphysical evolves the Astrophysical and from the Astrophysical evolves the physical one. Similarly, during the dissolution, the physical dissolves into the astrophysical, and the astrophysical finally dissolves into the metaphysical. Vedic scholiasts tried to define all three interdependent aspects through equivalence. That is why the terminology and terms applied by them have equivalence in the fields of adhyātma, adhidaivata and adhibhūta. The Vedic visionaries who visualised the laws of parā and aparā nature beyond time and space applied various methods to define the laws of parā nature (metaphysical) and aparā nature (astrophysical and physical sciences). All these methods were figurative, signifying adhyātma (metaphysical), adhidaivata (astrophysical) and adhibhūta (physical aspect). Yājñas were not the ends, but they were meant to elucidate and explain the physical, astrophysical and metaphysical intents of the Vedas. In fact, the metaphysical was the primary intent of the

Vedas, with astrophysical and physical intents being dealt with secondarily. Similarly, Brahmanic ritualism was subjected to adhyātma (metaphysical) as their primary significance and others such as adhidaivata (astrophysical) and adhibhūta (physical) are dealt with as the secondary significance. A close perusal of the Brāhmaṇas confirms this fact. The adhyātmika intent of the yajñas has been referred to 100 times therein, while astrophysical and physical intents have been referred to 60 times and 9 times, respectively (for detail, see RPA, 1991, 59-60).

In addition to this, hosts of instances may be cited where the yajñas can be shown to have been intended by authors of the Brāhmaṇas for representing the knowledge of adhyātma. For instance, the *Ś.Br.* 10.2.5.1 & 2 narrates the aim of the Agnicayana ceremony as to ātmasanskāra or self-purification:

तथैवैतद् यजमान एताः पुरः प्रपद्याभयेऽ नाष्ट्रा एतमात्मानं सन्स्कुरुते ।

tathaivaitad yajamāna etāḥ puraḥ prapadyābhaye' nāṣṭrā etamātmānaṁ sanskurute.

Confer Sāyana's commentary here:

तथाऽयं यजमानोऽपि उपसदोर्मध्ये अग्निचयनेनात्मानम् सन्स्कुरुते ।

tathā'yaṁ yajamāno'pi upasadormadhye agnicayanenātmānam sanskurute.

At another place the *Ś.Br.* describes all the yajñas aiming at ātmasampādana or self-accomplishment, e.g.

सर्वैर्हि यज्ञैरात्मानम् सम्पन्नम् विदे (१०.२.६.१५)

sarvairhi yajñairātmānam sampannam vide (10.2.6.15)

At yet another place Ś.Br. proclaims Agnihotra as the expounder of Ātman or Brahman, i.e., Supreme self, e.g.

शौचेयो ह प्राचिनयोग्य उद्दालकम् आरुणिमाजगां ब्रह्मोद्यं अग्निहोत्रं विविदिसिष्यामि इति । (११.५.३.१)

Śauceyo ha prācinayogya uddālakam āruṇimājagāṁ brahmodyaṁ agnihotraṁ vividisiṣyāmi iti. (11.5.3.1)

We come across a reference in Ś.Br. where Darśa-pūrṇamāsa and Cāturmāsya sacrifices are depicted as having twofold objects of their performance, viz. ātmayājītva (i.e. metaphysical or manifestations of self) and devayājītva (astrophysical), as in:

प्रजापतिरह चातुर्मास्यैरात्मानम् विदधे (११.५.२.१)

prajāpatiraha cāturmāsyairātmānam vidadhe (11.5.2.1)

Sāyana's commentary is noteworthy here. According to him,

यथा दर्शपूर्णमासयाजिन देवयाजित्वं चेति द्वैविध्यं दर्शितं एवं चातुर्मास्य याजिनोऽपि तथात्वं दर्शयितुं शरीरावयवकल्पनम् आख्यिकया रचयति ।

yathā darśapūrṇamāsayājina devayājitvaṁ ceti dvaividhyaṁ darśitaṁ evaṁ cāturmāsya yājino'pi tathātvaṁ darśayituṁ śarīrāvayavakalpanam ākhyikayā racayati.

Thereupon as regards the question as to who is superior between devayājī and ātmayājī Ś.Br. clarifies :

आत्मयाजी श्रेयान् देवयाजि इति, आत्मयाजीति स ह आत्मयजीनो वेदेदं मेऽनेनाङ्गम् सन्स्क्रीयते इदं मेऽनेनाङ्गम् उपधीयत इति. (११.२.६.२३)

ātmayājī śreyān devayāji iti, ātmayājīti sa ha ātmayajīno vededaṁ me'nenāṅgam sanskrīyate idaṁ me'nenāṅgam upadhīyata iti. (11.2.6.23)

That is, 'ātmayājī is superior between ātmayājī and devayājī. Ātmayājī is he who knows while performing yajña which part of his body is being consecrated or augmented by a particular action of yajña.'

Thus, the internal evidence of the Brāhmaṇas gives

support to the view that the ceremonial rituals of the Brāhmaṇas indicated physical, astrophysical and metaphysical meanings in order of preference.

Agniṣomīya paśuyāga (ASPY), being one in the series, also represents the metaphysical, astrophysical and physical aspects. In a metaphysical sense, it is charging an individuated consciousness with knowledge. Paśu here means a curious student or an individual (individuated consciousness) who can perceive the world around him but is devoid of knowledge or cognition. Paśu saṁjñapana means to make the individuated consciousness surcharged with knowledge. Complete surcharging leads to the universalization of consciousness or mokṣa from the physical body. Agni means a charge of knowledge or says a Guru or a teacher, and Soma is a good conductor of charge or, say, a student worthy of charging with knowledge. A Soma is constantly sacrificed to Agni to accomplish the process of surcharging. This subject has been handled in detail by Swami Dayānanda Saraswati while rendering his interpretation of Yajurveda. Here, knowledge is the property of ātman or consciousness, and until and unless the consciousness is completely surcharged with knowledge, it cannot attain universal hood or mokṣa. The seers had it as :

ऋते ज्ञानात् न मुक्तिः ।

ṛte jñānāt na muktiḥ.

But here it may be pointed out that the Agniṣomīya paśuyāga has its equivalence at astrophysical as well as physical levels also. Physically, it represents the annihilation process of agneya (-vely charged particle) and somiya (+vely charged particle) matter or particles known in modern science as matter and anti-matter. Astrophysically, it represents the method of rain formation, which is the main subject of this chapter.

In fact, when the metaphysical aspect is signified, the yajñas assume the character of Brahmayajña; while signifying the astrophysical aspect, they are termed as Devayajñas. Thus, the Brahmayajña form of ASPY signifies the metaphysical aspect, and the Devayajña form of ASPY signifies the astrophysical sense. The purpose of the Devayajña form of ASPY is narrated in the Yajurveda mantra as follows:

अद्भ्यस्त्वौषधिभ्यः.... (यजु. ६.९)

adbhyas tauṣadhibhyaḥ.... (*VS.* 6.9)

That is, for the sake of waters and vegetation, we procure you O havis.

The same mantra further reads:

अनु त्वा माता मन्यताम् अनु पितानु भ्राता सगभर्योऽनु सखा सयूथ्यः. (६.९)

anu tvā mātā manyatām anu pitānu bhrātā sagarbhyo'nu sakhā sayūthyaḥ. (6.9)

'Let your parent herbs, sister herbs, and simultaneously born herbs and your friendly herbs permit you to be procured for rain and vegetation growth.'

During translating this stanza, Uvaṭa clarifies the same with a quotation from Śruti.

इदंहि यदावर्षत्यथ् औषधयो जायन्ते ।

idaṁhi yadāvarṣatyath auṣadhayo jāyante

'When it rains, herbs grow.'

Thus, the main purpose of Agniṣomīya paśu yāga in adhidaivata sense works out, as is evident from the actual verse of the VS. to be rainmaking. This is why the seer says that the paśu (vegetation) endowed with the quality of Agni and Soma is procured for yajña.

अग्रीषोमाभ्यां जुष्टं नि युनज्मि ॥ 6.9 ॥

अग्निषोमाभ्याम् जुष्टं नियुनज्मि (यजु. ६.९)

agniṣomābhyām juṣṭaṁ niyunajmi (VS. 6.9)

And the type of vegetation i.e. vegetation worthy of augmenting the power of Agni and Soma are consecrated. *Agniṣomābhyām tvājuṣṭaṁ prokṣāmi* (VS. 6.9). In fact, for making it rain, Agni and Soma are coordinated in a particular ratio.

अपां च ज्योतिषश्च मिश्रीभावकर्मणो वर्ष कर्म जायते।

apāṁ ca jyotiṣaśca miśrībhāvakarmaṇo varṣa karma jāyate

(See for detail RPA 1995: 146)

These two elements Agni and Soma are defined in Ś. Br. as under:

द्वयं वा इदं न तृतीयमस्ति। आर्द्रं चैव शुष्कं च। यच्छुष्कं तदाग्नेयं यदार्द्रं तत् सोम्यम्। (श.ब्रा. १.६.३.२३)

dvayaṁ vā idaṁ na tṛtīyamasti. ārdraṁ caiva śuṣkaṁ ca. yacchuṣkaṁ tadāgneyaṁ yadārdraṁ tat somyaṁ.

(*Ś.Br.* 1.6.3.23)

'There are only two elements. No third one is there. One is dry, and another is wet. Dryness pertains to Agni, and wetness pertains to Soma.'

Here the great debatable term is paśu. This yajña has primarily been taken by many ancient and modern Vedic scholiasts for animal killing. According to them, including Mahidhara, one of the commentators of VS., in ASPY animal is sacrificed. So, the tradition of animal sacrifice is also traced back to the Vedas.

In fact, scholars could not make out the actual intent

of paśu. So, they speculated paśu for its conventional sense, i.e., animal. Now, we shall try to ascertain the actual meaning of paśu intended by the seer on the basis of internal evidence of mantras implied in Agniṣomī ya paśuyā ga and their explanation in Ś.Br. in the course of handling the same subject. Ś.Br. (3.8.4.5) defines paśu broadly as life essence. This paśu is the oblation metaphysical for all devas (natural forces).

प्राण एव पशु: सर्वासां वै देवानां हवि: पशु:. (श.ब्रा. ३.८.४.५)

prāṇa eva paśuḥ sarvāsāṁ vai devānāṁ haviḥ paśuḥ.

(*Ś.Br.* 3.8.4.5)

A.Br. also points out that paṣu is the oblation material.

हविर्हि पशु: ।

havirhi paśuḥ

Now the question arises as to what was the actual nature of paśu to be sacrificed as the havi for deities in the context of Devayajña. Whether it was animals or plants. To clarify, we may quote the seer of the Yajurveda here. According to him, vanaspati or vegetation is selected for devayajña.

तं त्वा जुषामहे देव वनस्पते देवयज्यायै ॥5.42 ॥

taṁ tvā juṣāmahai deva vanaspate devayajñāyai.

(*VS. 5.42*).

'O vegetation, we select you as oblation-material for devayajña.'

Sacrificing material in devayajña is plants or foodgrains and nothing else; it is proved by the following reference of the *Ś.Br.* (1.2.1.20):

उलूखल मूसलाभ्यां दृषदुपलाभ्यां हविर् यज्ञं घ्नन्ति ।

ulūkhala mūsalābhyāṁ dṛṣadupalābhyāṁ havir yajñaṁ ghnanti.

'The sacrificing material for devayajña is pounded with the help of ulūkhala and mūsala (i.e. mortar and wooden pestle or grinding board and muller).'

Thus, the act of puśu's killing with ulūkhala and mūsala is, in fact, the preparation of havi to be offered to the fire of yajña.

घ्नन्ति वा एतत् पशुं यदग्नौ जुह्वति । (श.ब्रा. ३.८.१.१०)

ghnanti vā etat paśuṁ yadagnau juhvati.

(*Ś.Br.* 3.8.1.10)

At one another place Ś.Br. clearly, states that only vegetation is used for yajñas. Men could not have performed yajña but for vegetation. It is said that yajñas are performed only with vegetation.

वनस्पत्यो हि यज्ञिया । न हि मनुष्या यज्ञेरन् यद् वनस्पतयो न स्युः । तस्माद् आह वनस्पतिर् यज्ञिय इति ।

vanaspatyo hi yajñiyā. na hi manuṣyā yajñeran yad vanaspatayo na syuḥ. tasmād āha vanaspatir yajñiya iti.

The Śatpatha reference further makes it clear. Accordingly, by offering vegetation to yajñīya fire, we are not destroying them at all.

न वा एतं मृत्यवे नयन्ति यं यज्ञाय नयन्ति ।(श.ब्रा. ३.८.१.१०)

na vā etaṁ mṛtyave nayanti yaṁ yajñāya nayanti,

(*Ś.Br.* 3.8.1.10)

They cannot get eliminated by this way. In fact, they become imperishable. They again grow and get back to life (flourish) on the earth.

अमृतम् आयुर् हिरण्यम् । तद् अमृतं आयुंषि प्रतितिष्ठति । तथात उदेति । तथा सञ्जीवाति । (श.ब्रा. ३.८.१.१०)

amṛtam āyur hiraṇyaṁ. tad amṛtaṁ āyuṁṣi pratitiṣṭhati. tathāta udeti. tathā sañjīvāti. (Ś.Br. 3.8.1.10)

Not only the author of the Śatapatha, but the seer himself expresses nonetheless the similar view. He had it, as a result of yajña through the plants or foodgrains, rainy waters flow on the earth. These rainy waters will relieve you of the sin of cutting and destroying the vegetation since more and more vegetation will, in turn, be able to grow.

इदमापः प्र वहतावद्यं च मलं च यत् । यच्चाभिदुद्रोहानृतं यच्च शेपे अभीरुणम् । आपो मा तस्मादेनसः पवमानश्च मुंचतु ॥ 6.17 ॥

idamāpaḥ pravahatāvadyaṁ ca malaṁ ca yat. yaccābhi dudrohānṛtaṁ. yacca śepe abhīruṇam āpo mā tasmādenasaḥ pavamānañca muñcatu. (VS. 6.17)

Paśu was (anna) foodgrains. It is clearly indicated by Ś.Br. at one place as

न ह वा एतस्मा अग्रे पशवश्चक्षमिरे । यदन्नम् अभविष्यन् यथेयम् अन्नं भूता । (३.७.३.२)

na ha vā etasmā agre paśavaścakṣamire. yadannam abhaviṣyan yatheyam annaṁ bhūtā. (3.7.3.2)

'The paśus were therefore not able to see' in the beginning since foodgrains were called paśus.

Further, the seer tells us what sort of vegetation would be worthy of use as an Agniṣomīya paśu or material for offering as an oblation to ASPY.

According to the seer, the vegetation that has grown in water or has consumed a lot of water is worth being the deva havi (divine oblation) in Agniṣomīya paśuyāga.

अपां पेरुरस्यापो देवीः स्वदन्तु स्वात्तं चित्सद्देवहविः ।
सं ते प्राणो वातेन गच्छताँ समङ्गनि यजत्रैः सं यज्ञपतिराशिषा ॥10॥

apāṁ perūrasyāpo devīḥ svadantu svāttaṁ citsaddeva havīḥ. saṁ te prāṇo vātena gacchatāṁ sam aṅgāni yajatraiḥ saṁ yajña patirāśiṣā (*VS.* 6.10)

So, it must be made in mind that the have to be used for rainmaking or cloud-seeding should be of somī ya nature, i.e. it should have grown in a climate of high humidity and heavy rainfall.

Bṛhadāraṇyaka Upaniṣad also reflects an ample good light upon the rain-inducing effect of somīya āhutis, such as,

सोमं राजानं जुह्वति । तस्या आहूत्यै वृष्टिः संभवति ।

somaṁ rājānaṁ juhvati. tasyā āhūtyai vṛṣṭiḥ sambhavati.

(RPA 1995: 152)

This fact was proven during our experiments on rainmaking since all of our experiments for cloud-seeding and rainmaking were accomplished only with the help of Somī ya ā hutis. The author disclosed this fact in detail in his work Vedic Meteorology, part II, chapter 3.

Only somīya havis are not sufficed to induce rain or seed clouds, but they should be committed to the fire of yajña in the company of Ghṛta or fats obtained from the milk of a cow. The verse had it as:

घृतेनाक्तौ पशूँस्त्रायेथाँ रेवति यजमाने प्रियं धा आ विश।
उरोरन्तरिक्षात्सजूर्देवेन वातेनास्य हविषस्त्मना यज समस्य तन्वा भव। वर्षो
वर्षीयसि यज्ञे यज्ञपतिं धाः स्वाहा देवेभ्यो देवेभ्यः स्वाहा ॥6.11॥

ghṛtenāktau paśūṁs trāyethā revati yajamāne priyaṁ

*dhā   āviśa.   urorantarikṣātsajurdevena   vātenāsya
haviṣastinanā yaja somasya tanvā bhava. varṣo yajña-patim
dhāḥ svāhā devebhyo devebhyaḥ svāhā. (VS. 6.11)*

'Let the somīya āhutis be soaked in the Ghṛta.
Only after being soaked should they reach the
yajamāna. They should be offered to yajña in the
presence of air in the open sky. This way, they get
expanded in volume. Since they are born in rain,
they will induce rain. 'Let the yajamāna offer an
oblation in the name of the concerned deity or to
augment the power of the concerned deity.'

Not only somīya havis are soaked in Ghṛta, but the
oblations of a fairly good amount of Ghṛta is also offered
in this yajña.

घृतस्य कुल्या उप ऋतस्य पथ्या अनु ॥*12*॥

ghṛtasya kulyā upartasya pathyā anu. (VS. 6.12)

In our rainmaking experiments, we discovered that
Ghee is also one of the ingredients to be offered to the
fire of the yajña for rainmaking. The seer has visualised
this fact thousands of years ago.

After prescribing the offered material consisting of
Ghee and other somīya vegetation, the seer extols the
quality of celestial waters or water vapours abiding in
mid-sphere and seeks the ability to procure them. For
example,

देवीरापः शुद्धा वोद्व॒ः सुपरिविष्टा देवेषु सुपरिविष्टा वयं परिवेष्टारो
भूयास्म ॥6.13 ॥

*devirāpaḥ śuddhā vodhvaṁ supariviṣṭā deveṣu
supariviṣṭā vayaṁ pariveṣṭāro bhūyāsma. (VS. 6.13)*

'The celestial waters are pure and exist everywhere

in the upper region. They have found their place among other devas, i.e., Indra etc. Let us become capable of nabbing them or procuring them.'

In the next verse, each and every part of the havi is purified so that it may become worthy to be offered as an oblation.

वाचं ते शुन्धामि प्राणं ते शुन्धामि चक्षुस्ते शुन्धामि ॥6.14॥

vācaṁ te śundhāmi prāṇaṁ te śundhāmi, cakṣuste śundhāmi. (VS. 6.14)

Further, it was prayed that each and every part of the oblation material should be in a sound condition. For example, the seer likes it to be as:

मनस्त आप्यायतां वाक आप्यायतां प्राणस्त आप्यायतां चक्षुस्त आप्यायताँ श्रोत्रं त आप्यायताम्। यत्ते क्रूरं यदास्थितं तत्त आप्यायतां निष्ट्यायतां तत्ते शुध्यतु शमहोभ्यः।

manas ta āpyāyatāṁ vāk ta āpyāyatāṁ prāṇas ta āpyāyatāṁ cakṣus ta āpyāyatāṁ śrotraṁ ta āpyāyatāṁ yatte kruraṁ yadāsthitaṁ tat ta āpyāyatāṁ niṣṭyāyatāṁ tat te śudhyatu samahobhyaḥ. (VS. 6.15)

Thus, it is apparent from the foregoing that oblation-material should be pure and in a sound condition. There should be no impurity; it should not be in a decayed position. For this purpose, he asks the plant to provide the offering material intact. *oṣadhe trāyasva* (VS. 6.15). He further suggests not wrecking the plant with the cutting knife or sword. *svadhite mainaṁ hiṁsiḥ.* (6.15)

In the beginning, the seer has advised not to go for impure or mixed material. Still, in spite of all the care duly taken in selecting the somīya offering, there is the possibility of some material not being somīya and so creating the anti-rain effect. In such conditions, this type of material may necessarily be separated or removed. The seer explains this operation as follows:

रक्षसां भागोऽसि निरस्तँ रक्ष इदमहँ रक्षोऽभि तिष्ठामीदमहँ रक्षोऽव बाध इदमहँ रक्षोऽधमं तमो नयामि ।

rakṣasāṁ bhāgo' si nirastaṁ rakṣa idam ahaṁ takṣa'bhitiṣṭhāmidamahaṁ takṣo' vabādham idamahaṁ takṣa' dhamaṁ tamo nayāmi. (VS. 6.16)

'You create anti effects. I remove you since you are anti-material. I remove this anti-material. I stop this to be used. I throw it to the heap of rubbish.'

He also discloses the process as to what happens after somīya āhutis are offered to fire.

According to him, on being sacrificed, the āhuti goes to the upper layer of the atmosphere, and the air drifts upward on account of the heating effect of the yajñīya fire.

स्वाहाकृते ऊर्ध्वनभसं मारुतं गच्छतम् ॥6.16 ॥

svāhākṛte ūrdhvaṁ nabhasaṁ mārutaṁ gacchatam.

(*VS.* 6.16)

In fact, the Āhuti goes to the sky in the form of its essence or vapours, its carbon part scatters on the earth.

दिवं ते धूमो गच्छतु स्वज्योर्तिः पृथिवीं भस्मनाऽऽपृण स्वाहा ॥6.21 ॥

divaṁ te dhūmo gacchatu svar jyotiḥ pṛthivī bhasmanā pṛṇa svāhā. (VS. 6.21)

Thus, the āhutis reach their concerned deities in the form of smoke.

In the end, the purpose of Agniṣomīya paśuyāga is further explained by the seer's prayer to Varuṇa for releasing waters and herbs from their respective places of origin instead of destroying them. He asks for a pardon because though the herbs were not worth destroying, but they had been destroyed by sacrificing into the fire. He prays further, 'Let these waters and herbs be useful for us, let them be harmful to those who are harmful to us.' The stanza reads as follows:

माऽपो मौषधीर्हि ꣳ सीर्धार्म्नो धार्म्नो राजँस्ततो वरुण नो मुंच । यदा हुरघ्या इति वरुणेति शपामहे ततो वरुण नो मुंच । सुमित्रिया न आप ओषधयः सन्तु दुर्मित्रियास्तस्मै सन्तु योऽस्मान्द्वेष्टि यं च वयं द्विष्मः ॥6.22 ॥

māpo mauṣadhirhiṁsī dhāmno dhāmno rājanstato varuṇa no muñca yadāhuraghnyā iti varuṇeti śapāmahe tato varuṇa no muñca sumitriyā na āpa oṣadhayaḥ santu durmitriyastasmai santu yo asmāndveṣṭi yaṁ ca vayaṁ dviṣmaḥ. (*VS.* 6.22)

> 'Let the waters and herbs be not destroyed. Let them flourish at the respective places of their origin. Let the Varuṇa release them for us from the respective places of their origin. They are said not to be worth destroying, and we are blamed to have destroyed them. So please, O Varuṇa, excuse us. Let both the waters and herbs be friendly (useful) with us; let them be unfriendly with those harmful to us and who (bacteria) we want to destroy.'

This stanza marks the end of Agniṣomīya paśuyāga. Thus, it is crystal clear from the aforementioned discussion that the aim of Agniṣomīya paśuyāga is rainmaking or cloud-seeding so far as its astrophysical intent is concerned.

This yāga has nothing to do with animal sacrifice as proposed by ancient commentators of Yajurveda, like Uvaṭa, Mahīdhara and several modern occidentals and oriental scholars. In fact, the use of the word paśu creates this type of misconception in the mind of the readers.

They are misled by puśu, taking it to mean animal, but the actual intent of paśu here is the vegetation to be offered as an oblation to the fire.

हविर्हि पशुः ।

havirhi paśuḥ

Moreover, one should not forget that the seer of Yajurveda himself declares that vanaspati or vegetation is used for devayajña.

तं त्वा जषामेहे देव वनस्पते देवयज्यायै ॥5.42 ॥

tam tvā juṣāmahe deva vanaspate deva yajñāyai.
(VS. 5.42)

So far as the various parts to be offered to the fire of yajña are concerned, they fit suitably more in the context of ādhyātmika sense than in the astronomical sense.

REFERENCES

Ravi Prakash Arya (RPA), Researches into Vedic and Linguistic Studies, Grantha Bharati Prakashan, Delhi, 1991.

Uvaṭa and Mahīdhara, *Vājasaneyi Samhitā* (VS). Motilal Banarsidass, Varanasi.

Śatapatha Brāhmaṇa (Ś.Br.), Rashtriya Sanskrit Sansthan, Delhi, 1990.

The Somayāga

A Process of Rainformation

As it has been repeatedly stated by the present author, various Vedic Śrauta yajñas, starting from Agnyādhāna to the yajñas running into 1000 years, explain/represent, in an astrophysical sense, the various phases of the process of physical or astrophysical creation that going to last till 1000 Caturyugas or Mahāyugas, i.e. 311 billion years. In a spiritual sense, the same yajñas represent the process of emancipation of souls in this universe. For instance, in a spiritual sense, Agnyādhyāna explains/represents the existence of ātman, and in an astrophysical sense, the same represents the first origin of āgneya or fire element on the earth. In a physical sense, it represents the origin of the first charged particles from the energy. Agnihotra, in a spiritual sense, explains/represents the oblations of soma or prakṛti (matter) element on the puruṣa/agni (consciousness) element. In the astrophysical sense, it represents the change of day and night. In a physical sense, it represents the creation of matter from energy. Similarly, Darśapūrṇamāsa explains/ represents the change of fortnights, Cāturmāsya explains/represents the seasonal changes, and Gavāmayana explains/represents changes in winter and summer solstices, i.e. Uttarāyaṇa and Dakṣiṇāyana on the earth. Similarly, Agni-somīya-paśuyāga explains the operation for rainmaking, whereas Somayāga explains/represents the process/phenomenon of rain formation on the earth.

Somayāga: To start with, it is necessary to inform you that there are two types of yāgas, Śrauta yāgas and Smārta yāgas. Smārta yāgas have been described in Gṛhya Sūtras in the name of Various Sanskāras. They are called

Pākasanstha, because they end with some preparations. Śrauta yāgas have been described in Śrauta Sūtras. They are called Havisanstha and somasanstha. Havisanstha are those that end with oblations of puroḍāśa (vegetation in their ripened form) into the fire of Yajña (annihilation of particles and anti-particles in the physical sense). Somasanstha are those that end with oblations of soma (essence or juice of vegetation) into the fire. Puroḍāśa represents vegetation, herbs or particles, and soma represents the juice of vegetation (electrical charge in the physical sense). In fact, Somasanstha yāgas represent the conversion of energy into matter in the universe, whereas Havisanstha yāgas represent the conversion of matter into energy or annihilation of matter and anti-matter in the physical sense. It represents some operation carried out by human beings to bring about desired changes in the environment or, say, for modifying the environment according to the needs and requirements of animate beings on the earth. Havisanstha yāgas are of seven types viz. Agnyādheya, Agnihotra, Darśa, Pauraṇamāsa, Āgrayaṇa, Cāturmāsya and Paśubandha. Thus, all Paśuyāgas are included in Havisanstha Somayāgas. Here, it may also be known that in the Havisanstha Somayāgas, the term Paśu doesn't signify a conventional sense of animal, but a 'havi' or 'oblation' prepared especially for some targeted devatā, in general, is called Paśu. In a physical sense, it represents a charged particle. Similarly, Sautrāmaṇī Iṣṭi is also a form of Havisanstha Somayāga. Soma-sanstha Somayāgas are also of seven types. They are known as Agniṣṭoma, Atyagniṣṭoma, Ukthya, Śoḍasi, Vājapeya, Atirātra, Āptoryāma and Aṣṭaka.

Somayāga is started with agniṣṭoma yāga, which is accomplished within six days. On the First-day dikṣaṇīyeṣṭi is performed. This indicates the dikṣā or initiation of Yajamāna and his wife for the Somayāga. Since the Somayāga, in an astrophysical sense, represents the process of rain formation on the earth, the initiation of yajamāna and his wife is essential. The process of rain formation is accomplished with the help of agni and soma.

अपां च ज्योतिषश्च मिश्रीभावकर्मणो वर्ष कर्म जायते ।

apāṁ ca jyotiṣaśca miśrībhāvakarmaṇo varṣa karma jāyate. (RPA:146).

These two elements Agni and Soma are defined in the *Ś. Br.* (1.6.3.23) as under:

द्वयं वा इदं न तृतीयमस्ति । आर्द्रं चैव शुष्कं च । यच्छुष्कं तदाग्नेयं यदार्द्रं तत् सोम्यम् ।

dvayaṁ vā idaṁ na tṛtīyamasti. ārdraṁ caiva śuṣkaṁ ca. yacchuṣkaṁ tadāgneyaṁ yadārdraṁ tat somyaṁ.

'There are only two elements; there is no third one. One is dry, and the other is wet. Dryness pertains to Agni, and wetness pertains to Soma.'

Here, yajamāna represents agni, and his wife represents soma, so initiation of both is essential for this yāga to take place.

The next three days are devoted to the observance of Iṣṭis and Pravargay. Fifth-day soma is procured, and Somayāga is accomplished in three phases: prātaḥ savana (in the morning hours), mādhyandina savana (during noon) and sāyaṁ savana (evening hours). These three phases represent the three phases of a year, each consisting of 4 months (Chāturmāsya), the first phase being the rainy season, the second phase being the winter season, and the third phase the summer season. The Sixth-day closing is marked with the avabhṛtha rite.

In this yāga, which is accomplished in three phases/seasons of 4 months each (represented respectively by three days, i.e. 4th, 5th and 6th day), three types of paśus are procured in each phase. The first phase, representing the rainy season, consists of 4 months (Chāturmāsya), represented by the fourth day of yāga, agniṣomīya paśu (that is, rain-bearing monsoon formed of āgneya and somīya elements) is procured.

On the fifth day, representing the second phase of the winter season consisting of 4 months (Chāturmāsya), savanīya paśu (seeded cloud that delivers rain in the rainy season) is procured.

On the sixth day, representing the third phase of the summer season consisting of 4 months (Chāturmāsya), *maitrāvāruṇī vāśā anubandhyā gau* (vaporisation caused by Mitra and Varuṇa which is not capable of delivering rain) is procured.

The Somayāga is accomplished with the following ceremonial acts.

1. Pravargya

In the pravargya ceremony, ghee is heated in an earthen pot and mixed with the milk of a cow or goat. The heating of ghee in this ceremony symbolises the radiation heating of the earth in the summer season, and the pouring of milk symbolises the evaporation of waters that takes place due to radiation heating.

2. Purchase of Soma

The next ceremony is to purchase the Soma from *Ekahāyanī Aruṇā gau*. Here, eka (one) hāyana represents one year, and aruṇā gau represents the red-hued lightning of the clouds. This ceremony indicates that soma (rainy waters) are received from the red-hued lightning occurring in the rainy season after one year. The different hues of lightning herald different met phenomenon. For example:

वाताय कपिला विद्युदात्पायातिलोहिनि कृष्णा सर्वनाशाय दुर्भिक्षाय सिता भवेत् ।

vātāya kapilā vidyudātpāyātilohini kṛṣṇā sarvanāśāya durbhikṣāya sitā bhavet.

That is kapilā (yellow) coloured lightning signals storms and cyclones, violet coloured calls for very heat. The black hue signals destruction and the white coloured points out the famine.

3. Agniṣomīya Paśu

Agniṣomīya paśu is nothing but the maritime winds (blowing from sea to continents) are called somīya paśu and continentals winds (blowing from dry reasons) are called as āgneya paśu. In fact, air/the wind, fire and the sun have been described as paśu in the Yajurveda. For example, Yajurveda (23.17) says:

अग्नि पशुर् आसीत्, तेनायजन्त, वायु पशुर् आसीत् तेनायजन्त, सूर्यः पशुर् आसीत् तेनायजन्त ।

agni paśur āsīt, tenāyajanta, vāyu paśur āsīt tenāyajanta, sūryaḥ paśur āsīt tenāyajanta.

That is in the process of creation (adhidaivika yajña) fire acted as paśu (animal) to be offered as an oblation. Similarly, wind/air acted as an animal which was also sacrificed and the sun also acted as paśu and so was also sacrificed as an oblation. This means to say that the physical creation evolved out of the fire, air and sun.

Thus, Agniṣomīya paśu refers to the monsoon winds or other winds capable of bringing rain.

4. Havirdhāna Maṇḍapa

Havirdhāna maṇḍapa signifies the place where the havis escaped. In the astronomical context of Somayāga, mid sphere or antarikṣa acts as the havirdhāna maṇḍapa where the evaporated waters (soma) are located. Soma (evaporated waters) are the oblations of Somayāga. Here, it may be informed that pavamāna soma is a deity in the Vedas, which signifies rainy or evaporated waters. These somas are called as pavamāna as they are distilled or purified waters. The ancient Vedic scholar Yāska reads the term havi in the names of clouds. Accordingly, in Somayāga, evaporated waters condensed into clouds act as havi.

5. Havirdhāna Śakaṭa (Cart carrying havis)

In Somayāga, there are two havirdhāna śakaṭas placed in opposite directions of south and north. These two carts carrying havis (oblations of soma for somayāga) are nothing but clouds floating in opposite directions carrying the evaporated waters. The opposite flow of these clouds makes them oppositely charged. Here, it may be recalled that precipitation occurs when oppositely charged clouds in the mid-sphere are discharged. To explain the above phenomenon of rain formation, two carts bearing havis are placed in opposite directions in Somayāga.

6. Soma Abhiṣava (Delivery of rain)

In Somayāga, soma abhiṣava (soma extraction) is enacted with the help of two stones (mortar and pestle) called grāvā. Vegetation or herb is crushed with the help of two grāvā to extract soma. This process of crushing with the help of two grāvās (stones) is followed by a sound. In the Vedic tradition, grāvā signifies cloud and not stone. This is clear from Nighaṇṭu. Yāska, in his

Nighaṇṭu, reads terms like grāvā, adri, etc., that denote stone in the conventional sense to signify clouds. Thus, the act of crushing of soma with the help of two grāvā in the Somayāga signifies the discharging of two oppositely charged clouds, contact of which produces a short circuit and unleashes a high amplitude current called lightning followed by acoustic shock waves, which are represented here in Somayāga by the sound produced by two grāvās. The following mantra of Parjanya Sūkta of Ṛgveda (5.83.2) describes the power of such shock waves as viśvaṁ vibhāya bhuvanaṁ mahāvadhāt-the entire universe got frightened with the shocking sound caused by the contact of oppositely charged clouds. This process of discharging between oppositely charged clouds leads to the precipitation of rain, known as soma or Pavamāna soma in the Vedas. The same phenomenon of precipitation of rain has been described very amicably in the Ṛgveda (1.32.11) as:

दासपत्नीर् अहिगोपा अतिष्ठन् निरुद्धाः आपः पणिनेव गावः ।
अपां बिलम् अपिहितम् यदासीत् वृत्रं जघन्वान् अप तद् ववार ।।

dāsapatnīr ahigopā atiṣṭhan
niruddhāḥ āpaḥ paṇineva gāvaḥ.
apāṁ bilam apihitam yadāsīt
vṛtraṁ jaghanvān apa tad vavāra.

That is, the waters hidden in the clouds were allowed to fall as rainy waters due to the discharging of oppositely charged clouds.

7. Placement of Adhiṣavaṇaphalaka (Wooden board)

The mortar (stone) upon which soma extraction is done is supported by a wooden board called adhiṣavaṇa phalaka. This wooden board is called adhiṣavaṇa because of the etymology '*adhiṣūyate asmin iti adhiṣavaṇa.*' That is, it's the basis of soma extraction. The wooden board represents the layer of the troposphere, which is the basis of cloud formation and rain precipitation.

8. Digging of Uparavas (pits)

Uparavas are a sort of pit that is dug underneath the havirdhāna śakaṭa (havi-bearing cart). They are four in number. They are dug so that they appear separated externally but remain one internally. They are covered with two wooden boards. This all symbolises the four different months making one single ṛtu/rain season. The covering by two wooden boards symbolises the covering of four months of rainy season by two types of clouds (-vely and +vely charged clouds).

9. Three Savanas

The Somayāga is accomplished in three savanas, viz. prātaḥ (morning) savana, mādhyandin (noon) savana and sāyaṁ (evening) savana. These three savanas denote three seasons of the year, i.e. rainy, winter and summer. Prātaḥ savana denotes the rainy season, Mādhyandin savana denotes the winter season and sāyaṁ savana denotes the summer season since somayāga gives an account of the distribution of rain throughout the year divided into three seasons of four months each.

10. Distribution of Soma in various savanas

The total amount of soma to be extracted is divided into two parts: a larger and a smaller. The Larger amount is extracted in the morning savana, and the smaller amount is extracted in the noon savana. The pulp of both extractions is again crushed in the evening savana for extraction of soma. This process indicates that precipitation occurs in large amounts on the earth during the rainy season, which is reduced in the winter. It hardly takes place in the summer season. Thus, Somayāga points out the distribution of rainy water (Pavamāna soma) on the earth throughout the year divided into three seasons of four months each.

11. Savanīya Paśu (Animal)

Savanīya paśu is nothing but the seeded cloud. A seeded cloud is called savanīya because it becomes worthy of inducing rain. The tallow of the Savanīya paśu is sacrificed in the morning savana. The tallow of Savanīya paśu (cloud) is nothing but the precipitation. The morning savana symbolises, as indicated earlier, the rainy season. By sacrificing the tallow of savanīya paśu, the seer wants to tell that clouds in the rainy season induce the rain. Puroḍāśa is sacrificed in the noon hour (mādhyandin savana). Puroḍāśa symbolises hailstorms. Hailstorms take place in the noon hour, i.e. winter season. In the evening hour, the body parts of savanīya paśu are sacrificed. The body parts symbolise the remaining parts of clouds that yield rain in the summer season.

12. Anubandhyā Maitrāvaruṇī Vaśā

On the Sixth day or the last day, Maitrāvaruṇī vaśā is sacrificed in the Yajña. Here, it may be pointed out that most scholars take vaśā for the meaning of a 'barren cow'. No doubt, vaśā stands for 'barren', but it is absurd to use the suffix cow in the expression vaśā. Since nowhere vaśā has been attributed to gau or cow. In this yāga also, maitrāvaruṇī vaśā is mentioned. Mitra and Varuṇa are the rainmaking agents. The Vedic seer proclaims, *mitrāvaruṇau tvā vṛṣṭyāvatam*. (VS. 2.16) 'May the Mitra and Varuṇa bring rain for you.

मित्रावरुणौ वृष्ट्याधिपति तौ मावताम् । अथर्ववेद, 5.24.5

Mitrāvaruṇau vṛṣṭyādhipati tau māvatām. (AV. 5.24.5)

May the rainmaking agents Mitra and Varuṇa protect you.

In fact, the coordination of both elements was considered necessary for inducing rain, and the proposed coordination could easily be affected with the help of Yajña.

यज्ञा नो मित्रावरुणा यज्ञा देवं ऋतं बृहत् ।

yajñā no mitrāvaruṇā yajñā devaṁ ṛtaṁ bṛhat.

'Mitra and Varuṇa, the main agents of rain, should be co-ordinated with the help of Yajña for rain precipitation.'

We have read above that on the savanīya day (fifth day), the savanīya paśu or seeded cloud was sacrificed to induce rain. After the rainy season, seeded clouds no longer exist, and the existing clouds cannot precipitate since clouds are formed of Mitra and Varuṇa elements. Thus, the remaining maitrāvaruṇī elements (clouds) are known as vaśā or barren ones since the clouds are not able to precipitate in the winter season. Unravelling the secrets of maitrāvaruṇī vaśā (clouds composed of Mitra and Varuṇa elements but not able to precipitate for want of the required amount of evaporated waters) Śatpatha Brāhmaṇa (4.5.1.9) says:

अथ यदा न कश्चन रसः पर्यशिष्यत् तत् एषा मैत्रावरुणी वशा समभवत्. तस्माद् एषा न प्रजायते. रसाद्धि रेतः सम्भवति रेतसः पशवः ।

atha yadā na kaścana rasaḥ paryaśiṣyat tat eṣā maitrāvaruṇī vaśā samabhavat. tasmād eṣā na prajāyate. rasāddhi retaḥ sambhavati retasaḥ paśavaḥ.

'When no water drops are left there, the clouds are known as maitrāvaruṇī vaśā. Since those clouds (maitrāvaruṇī vaśā) are not able to precipitate, the rain or rainy water (rasa) causes the production of retas (seaman), and living beings are born of retas.'

Finally, the Śatapatha Brāhmaṇa (4.5.1.9) illustrates the reason as to why this vaśā is sacrificed at the end of the yāga. Accordingly:

तद् यद् अन्ततः समभवत् । तस्मादन्तं यज्ञस्य अनुवर्तते ।

tad yad antataḥ samabhavat. tasmādantaṁ yajñsya anuvartate.

'Because the maitrāvaruṇī vaśā is left at the end of yajña (phenomenon) of rain formation, that is why here also in Somayāga, the maitrāvaruṇī vaśā is sacrificed at the end.'

Hope now the readers/scholars can know the mystery of Somayāga. We all must keep in mind that Vedic knowledge cannot so easily be comprehended. It's not a layman's literature. To understand the Vedas, it is essential to understand the cultural background of the Vedas and the intricacies of the grammar and style of the Vedic Language. Unravelling this mystery, the Brāhmaṇakāras say,

परोक्षप्रिया इव हि देवाः प्रत्यक्ष द्विषः ।

parokṣapriyā iva hi devāḥ pratyakṣa dviṣaḥ

I.e. Vedic seers like to describe the knowledge in the secondary (prokṣa) sense, and they have an aversion to relating the mystery in the primary (pratyakṣa) sense.

Later on, this method of describing the matter in a secondary sense (taddhitārtha) was given a grammatical colouring. Secondary suffixes were used with the original words to convey the secondary sense. Yāska, an ancient Vedic scholar, has unfolded this intricacy of Vedic language, illustrating an example. At Nirukta (2.1), in the context of the Vedic expression 'gau' Yāska says:

गौर् इति पृथिव्या नामधेयम्। यद् दूरङ्गता भवत्.................अथाप्यस्यां ताद्धितेन कृत्स्नवत् निगमा भवन्ति 'गोभिः श्रीणीत मत्सरम्। अंशु दुहन्तोऽध्यासते गवि इति अधिषवणचर्मणः।

gaur iti pṛthivyā nāmadheyam. yad dūraṅgatā bhavat.................athāpyasyāṁ tāddhitena kṛtsnavat nigamā bhavanti 'gobhiḥ śriṇīta matsaram'. aṁśu duhanto'dhyāsate gavi iti adhiṣavaṇacarmaṇaḥ.

Gau is the name of the earth in the astronomical (adhidaivika) sense since it goes far away while orbiting the sun. This gau is also used in laukika (conventional) sense to mean laukika gau or 'cow' since the cow is also used to go far off places while grazing. The expression 'gau' in the Vedas, while denoting 'laukika gau' or cow, implies a secondary sense. For instance, in the expression '*gobhiḥ śriṇīta matsaram*' 'go' has been used in the secondary sense. Its primary (pratyakṣa) meaning is 'cow', and its secondary (prokṣa) meaning is 'product of cow' Here, the expression gau signifies 'product of cow' or say *gopayobhiḥ* (cow milk) and not 'go' 'cow' herself. So, the meaning of the above phrase will be 'Cook soma' (herbs/vegetables) with cow milk. Similarly, the phrase '*adhyāste gavi*' (literally meaning 'sits on the cow') also does not signify the primary sense 'sits on the cow', but the meaning of the above phrase will be 'sits on the leather of cow.

Thus, having illustrated these two examples, Yāska there itself clarifies that the names of other animals also create similar doubts in the Vedas and allied literature.

एवम् अन्येषाम् अपि सत्त्वानां सन्देहाः विद्यन्ते।

evam anyeṣām api sattvānāṁ sandehāḥ vidyante.

Yāska here clearly mentions that when Vedic expressions apply to laukika (conventional) things or animals, etc., they signify a secondary sense and not the primary sense as generally held by the scholars. But when they apply to ādhyātmika (spiritual) objects like mind, spirit, God, etc. or astronomical objects like stars and planets, they are used in primary meaning. For example, the expression 'gau' if it applies to spiritual objects like sense-organs and astronomical objects like the earth is always used in the primary meaning, but if the same expression 'gau' applies to laukika or an earthly object like 'cow' is mainly used in the secondary purport. Here, I would quote a fascinating example from Śatpatha Brāhmaṇa (3.4.1.2) in the context of entertaining a guest. This phrase has also appeared in several Gṛhya Sūtras as quoted by Jha (51, footnote 72), according to the reference of Ś.Br. (3.4.1.2) The deities are entertained with the help of havis, and the guests are entertained with the help of grains produced by bulls and milk produced by goats. Here, the Brāhmaṇakāra says:

यथा राज्ञे वा ब्राह्मणाय वा महोक्षं वा महाजं वा पचेत् तदाह मानुषं हविर् देवानाम् एवमस्मा एतदातिथ्यं करोति ।

yathā rājñe vā brāhmaṇāya vā mahokṣaṁ vā mahājaṁ vā pacet tadāha mānuṣaṁ havir devānām evamasmā etadātithyaṁ karoti.

Just as a king or a renowned scholar is entertained with the recipes of grains produced by a strong bull or of the milk produced by a healthy goat respectively. This was the method of entertaining human guests. Similarly, the astronomical guests or natural powers called devas are entertained by the oblations offered to the yajñīya fire.

Here, several scholars translate mahokṣaṁ as a big bull and mahājam as a big goat. Similarly, the words mahokṣam and mahājam occurred in other Gṛhyasūtras are also taken to mean big bulls and big goats. The translators forget that these expressions are not to be taken in their primary senses but then in the secondary sense (taddhitārtha), and accordingly, the mahokṣa and mahāja will signify recipes made of the grains produced by big bulls and milk produced by big healthy goats. Following the similar notion prevalent about the Vedic language, it would be highly objectionable if a scholar without knowing the actual tendency and peculiarity of the Vedic language uses such phrases in a primary sense when they apply to laukika (conventional) objects. Such a scholar not only supports the inhumane killing of innocent animals but is also guilty of killing the Vedas and their actual intended sense.

So, with this detailed discussion held above, the author of the present lines thinks that some human sense would prevail upon so-called historians like D. N. Jha and others who are all out to uproot the glorious past of India and the entire earth inhabited by Vedic people.

References

1. Atharvaveda, ed. Devi Chand, Munshi Ram Manohar Lal, Delhi, 1982

2. Arya, Ravi Prakash (RPA), Vedic Meteorology, Delhi, 1995,

3. Jha, D.N. The Myth of the Holy Cow, Verso, London, 2002

4. Nirukta of Yāska, ed. with Sanskrit translation, Brahma Muni Parivrajaka.

5. Śatpatha Brāhmaṇa, with Sayana Bhaṣya, Nag Publication, Delhi.

Puruṣa-Medha
The Active Energy of Bhūtākāśa (Physical Space)

In the Vedas, the active energy of Bhūtākāśa observable space is called Puruṣa which is the life principle of the Universe. The *Chāndogya Upaniṣad*, compares Puruṣa with the Bhūtākāśa called universe. The *Śatapatha Brāhmaṇa* (13.6.2.21) also observes in the same manner as:

इमे वै लोकाः पूः। अयम् एव पुरुषो योऽपवते। सोऽस्यां पुरि शेते तस्मात् पुरुषः। यदेषु लोकेष्वन्नं तदस्यान्न मेधः। तद्-यद् अस्य्-ऐतद् अन्नं मेधस् तस्मात् पुरुष्मेधः। अथो यदस्मिन् मेध्यान् पुरुषा नालभते तस्माद् एव पुरुष-मेधः।

ime vai lokāḥ pūḥ, ayam eva puruṣo yo'pavate. so'syaṁ puri śete tasmāt puruṣaḥ. yadeṣu lokeṣvannaṁ tadasyānnaṁ medhaḥ. tad-yad asy-aitad annaṁ medhas tasmāt puruṣmedhaḥ. atho yadasmin medhyān puruṣā nālabhate tasmād eva puruṣa-medhaḥ

[Meaning] This bhūtākāśa is like the physical body. One who resides in this body is called Puruṣa (Note active energy resides in this bhūtākāśa). Active energy in the universe acts as food since this food is consumed for the evolution of the universe. That is why the Puruṣamedha (evolution of the universe) takes place.

This puruṣmedha works on the principle of conversion of active energy of Bhūtākāśa into matter particles.

The *Charaka Saṁhitā* (*Śarīra-sthāna*, 5.3) describes

Puruṣa (the active energy of the bhūtākāśa the epitome of the Universe. The concept of 'Brahmāṇḍa Puruṣa' is the outcome of the above Vedic concept, which establishes a parallelism between the organic whole and the universal whole. यद् अण्डे तद् ब्रह्माण्डे *yad aṇḍe tad brahmāṇḍe.*

According to the *Puruṣa Śukta* of the *Ṛgveda* (10.90.10), the Puruṣa (active energy of bhūtākāśa) gives birth to four paśus: Avi, Aśva, Ajā and Gau in bhūtākāśa. The mantra reads as under:

तस्मादश्वा अजायन्त ये के चोभयादतः ।
गावो ह जज्ञिरे तस्मात्तस्माज्जाता अजावयः ॥ यजुर्वेद, 31.8

tasmādaśvā ajāyanta ye ke chobhayādataḥ,
gāvo ha jajñire tasmāttasmājjātā ajāvayaḥ.

[tasmāt] From that puruṣa, [aśvāḥ] light particles [ajāyanta] were produced [ye ke cha] which (ubhayādataḥ) behaved both like particles and waves; [tasmāt] from that puruṣa, [gāvaḥ] gau geothermal energy of planets [jañjīre] was created; [tasmāt] from the same yajña, [ajā] the black energy and [avi] field energy [jātāḥ] were formed.

Thus, Bhūtākāśa observable universe became conspicuous with the presence of four grāmya paśus like Aśva, Gau, Avi and Ajā. Here, Aśva represents stars or light particles, gau symbolises planets and satellites or geothermal energy, Avi represents intermediate space or field energy, and Aja is the black holes in the universe. These all-material bodies are the source of energy. For example, stars are the source of solar energy or light, planets are the source of geothermal energy and intermediate space is the source of field energy. This fact has been corroborated by the *Śatapatha Brāhmaṇa* (6.2.1.-4) as Prajāpati saw agni (energy) in paśus (matter particles). Therefore, they are called paśus. This also means that all matter particles are made up of energy particles (Note: The word paśu is derived from the root dṛś (paśya) 'to see'.)

The *Yajurveda* (23.17) describes Agni (energy) as 'paśu' (matter particles). The *Taittīriya Brāhmaṇa* (1.1.4.5) mentions paśus matter particles) as āgneya (made of energy particles). All these Vedic authorities confirm that the objects of Bhūtākāśa (observable space or universe) are made up of energy, and they generate energy. Thus, Puruṣamedha in ādhidaivika (astronomical) sense means conversion of active energy into matter particles in the Bhūtākāśa (observable universe).

Aśva-Medha Yāga

A Process of Harnessing Solar-energy

Aśva: The Solar Energy

The Aśva in the Vedas is described as one among the 4 grāmya paśus, already mentioned above. Aśva here is nothing but the sun which is the biggest source of energy in our universe. Ṛgveda (1.163.2) compares the sun with Aśva (horse). Taittirīya Brāhmaṇa (3.9.23.2) describes Aśva as āditya. Aitareya Brāhmaṇa (6.35) more emphatically mentions the radiant sun as white Aśva –

अथ योऽसौ (सूर्यः) तपती एषोऽश्वः श्वेतो रूपं कृत्वाऽश्वाभिधान्यपिहितेनात्मना प्रतिचक्राम ।

/atha yo'sau (suryaḥ) tapatī eṣo'śvaḥ śveto rūpaṁ kṛtvā'śvābhidhānyapihitenātmanā praticakrāma.

Gopatha Brāhmaṇa (Second part 3.19) also calls the sun Aśva—sauryyo vā aśvaḥ [Sun is verily Aśva]. In Vedic and Paurāṇika allegories, the sun is described as a chariot yoked with seven horses. These seven horses are nothing but the sun's seven vibgyor rays.

In the *Yajurveda*, (23.53), the following query has been raised.

का स्विद् आसीत् पूर्व-चित्तिः । किं स्विद् आसीद् बृहद् वयः । का स्विद् आसीत् पिलिप्पिला । का स्विद् आसीत् पिशिङ्गिला ।

kā svid āsīt pūrva-cittiḥ. kiṁ svid āsīd bṛhad vayaḥ. kā svid āsīt pilippilā. kā svid āsīt piśiṅgilā.

[Meaning] What is the first storehouse (of energy)?

What is the biggest source of energy in the Bhūtākāśa (observable space)? What object is pilippilā (protector) and what object is piśaṅgilā (devourer)?'

The answer given in the next mantra (Yajurveda, 23.54) is as under:

द्यौर् आसीत् पूर्वचित्तिर् अश्व आसीद् बृहद् वय: ।

अविरासीत् पिलिम्पिला, रात्रिर् आसीत् पिशङ्गिला ।

dyaur āsīt pūrvacittir aśva āsīd bṛhad vayaḥ. avirāsīt pilippilā, rātrir āsīt piśaṅgilā.

[Meaning] Chidākāśa (space of Brahman) is the first storehouse of energy. Aśva (stars/sun) is the biggest source of energy in the Bhūtākāśa (observable space). Avi (intermediate space or magnetosphere) is the protector, and ajā (active energy in Bhūtākāśa) is the devourer of the entire material world.

The word Aśvamedha is formed of two words, Aśva + medha. The meaning of Aśva has already been elaborated as the sun. Medha is derived from the root medhṛ 'to achieve' or 'to kill'. The process of medha involves the gain of matter and loss of energy and vice versa. Aśvamedha yāga is nothing but a process to harness solar energy to sustain life on earth. The *Ṛgveda* (2.167.1) speaks about harnessing the energy from the sun for useful technical applications. It also highlights Earth receiving energy from the sun as:

यमेन दत्तं त्रित एनम् आयुनग् इन्द्रं प्रथमो अध्यतिष्ठत् ।
गन्धर्वो अस्य रशनाम् अगृभ्णात् सूराद् अश्वं वसवो निरतष्ट ॥

yamena dattaṁ trita enam āyunag indraṁ prathamo

adhyatiṣṭhat

gandharvo asya raśanām agṛbhṇāt sūrād aśvaṃ vasavo nirataṣṭa.

[Meaning] (vasavaḥ) The scholars (nirataṣṭa) harness (aśvaṃ) energy from (sūrād) sun (yama) in a controlled manner (ayunak) and utilized for various technological purposes. The energy was first transformed into Indra (electricity) for its applied use. Gandharva (magnetosphere of the earth) (agṛbhṇāt) captured the (raśanām) reins (radiations) from (sūrād) the sun.

Śatapatha Brahmaṇa (9.4.2.18) says that Aśvamedha is the sun - असावाऽदित्यऽश्वमेधः (asāvā'ditya'śvamedhaḥ). At another place, the *Śatapatha Brahmaṇa* (10.6.5.8) says that Aśvamedha is performed by the radiation heating from the sun- *eṣa vā aśvamedho ya eṣa (sūryaḥ) tapati.* Śatapatha Brahmaṇa (11.2.5.4) also says that Aśvamedha is to be performed year after year.

Following rituals are involved in the performance of Aśvamedha yāga.

4.1 Year-long ritual

Aśvamedha yāga is performed for a duration of one year, which symbolizes Earth's revolution around the sun.

4.2 Emperor Chakravarti Samrāṭ)

Aśvamedha yāga can be performed only by an Emperor (Cakravrati Samrāṭ). Here, Chakravrati Samrāṭ is symbolic of the sun because the sun alone is the emperor of the Solar system.

4.3 Requirement of Horse

Such a horse is required for the ritual, and its forepart is black, and its back part is white, with a cart-shaped mark on its forehead. The horse of Aśvamedha yāga with the above features is symbolic of the Sun since out of 24 hours of a solar day, the first 12 hours are covered by night, and the second 12 hours are covered by day. The night is represented by a dark hue, and the day by white. The cart sign on the forehead of the horse of Aśvamedha yāga represents the twilight hours when the rays of the rising sun on the eastern horizon give an impression of a cart.

4.4 Rein of Horse

Aśvamedha yāga horse is supposed to have a rein measuring 12 to 13 aratnis (units). This measurement of 12 to 13 aratnis symbolizes 12 months or 13 months (in the case of an intercalary month) of a year. Clarified butter is applied to the horse's rein, which symbolizes the sun's luminosity.

4.5 Four queens of the Emperor

The Aśvamedha yāga is performed by a consecrated king and four queens. Here, the four queens of the king are symbolic of four directions. Mahiṣī (queen dowager) symbolises the Eastern direction. The Sun rises in this direction. That is why it is figuratively said in Śatapatha Brahmaṇa (13.5.2.2) that the phallus of a horse is placed in the lap of Mahiṣī queen-

निरायत्याश्वस्य शिश्रं महिष्युपस्थे निधत्ते वृषा वाजी रेतोधा रेतो दधात्विति ।

nirāyatyāśvasya śiśnam mahiṣyupasthe nidhatte vṛṣā vājī retodhā reto dadhātviti.

Queen Vallabhā or Vāvātā (favourite) is symbolic of

the western direction. As the sun sets in the west, it is allegorically mentioned that the sun rests or sleeps in the western direction. Due to this reason, the king performing Aśvamedha yāga is advised to take a nap, resting his head in the laps of Vallbhā or Vāvātā queen. Similarly, queens named Avallbhā or Parivṛktā (unfavourite) and Dūtaputrī or Pālāgalī (daughter of envoy) represent north and south directions, respectively, because these directions can have their contact with the sun only during Uttarāyaṇa (winter solstice) and Dakṣiṇāyana (summer solstice).

4.6 Horse's year-long wandering

The year-long wandering of the horse symbolises the earth's period of revolution around the sun.

4.7 Bodyguards of the horse

Sun rays are the representative bodyguards of the horse. The *Ṛgveda* (6.47.18) mentions tens of hundreds of rays of the sun - युक्ता हर्यश्शतादश *(yuktā haryaś śatādaśa)*.

4.8 Fastening of the horse with ropes

In the Aśvamedha yāga, the horse is fastened with ropes from all sides. This is symbolic of the sun being surrounded by rays. Some other animals are tied to the rope surrounding the horse, symbolising the planets attracted to the sun due to gravitational pull.

Thus, it is proved that Aśvamedha yāga is nothing but a process to harness solar energy to sustain life on the earth. The Ṛgveda (2.167.1) speaks about harnessing the energy from the sun for practical technical applications. It also highlights the earth receiving energy from the sun.

यमेन दत्तं त्रित एनम् आयुनग् इन्द्रं प्रथमो अध्यतिष्ठत्।

गन्धर्वो अस्य रशनाम् अगृभ्णात् सूराद् अश्वं वसवो निरतष्ट ॥

yamena dattaṁ trita enam āyunag indraṁ prathamo adhyatiṣṭhat
gandharvo asya raśanām agṛbhṇāt sūrād aśvam vasavo nirataṣṭa.

[Meaning] The scholars (vasavaḥ) harness energy from the sun in a controlled manner (yama) and utilized (ayunak) for various technological purposes. The energy was first transformed into Indra (electricity) for its applied use. Gandharva (earth's magnetosphere) captured the reins (radiations) from the sun.

The *RV.* (3.2.3) talks about the multiple technologies developed from solar energy for long-term benefits, as

क्रत्वा दक्षस्य तरुषो विधर्मणि देवासो अग्निं जनयन्त चित्तिभिः ।
रुरुचानं भानुना ज्योतिषा महामत्यं न वाजं सनिष्यन्नुप ब्रुवे ।।

kratvā dakṣasya taruṣo vidharmaṇi devāso agniṁ janayanta cittibhiḥ
rurucānaṁ bhānunā jyotiṣā mahāmatyaṁ na vājaṁ saniṣyannupa bruve

[Meaning] The scholars (endowed) with intelligence, harness solar energy powerful like stead for multiple technological uses in order to get efficiency in accomplishing their tasks.

The mantra clearly points out the development of affordable, inexhaustible and clean solar energy technologies which will have huge long-term benefits. It will increase the countries' energy security through reliance on an indigenous, inexhaustible and mostly import-independent resource, enhance sustainability, reduce pollution, and lower the cost of mitigating climate change.

As per modern estimates, the total solar energy absorbed by Earth's atmosphere, oceans and landmasses is approximately 3,850,000 exajoules (EJ) annually. In 2002, this was more energy in one hour than the world used in one year. Photosynthesis captures approximately 3,000 EJ per year in biomass. The amount of solar energy reaching the planet's surface is so vast that in one year, it is about twice as much as will ever be obtained from all of the Earth's non-renewable resources of coal, oil, natural gas and mined uranium combined. The scripture says- "*Sūrya ātmā jagatasthuśaś ca*" [The Sun is the soul of this world, animate and inanimate].

Go-Medha

The Geothermal Energy

The Vedic seers were well aware of geothermal energy. The *Śatapatha Brāhmaṇa* (14.9.4.19) says that the earth holds energy in her womb. This fact is clarified more vividly in the *Yajurveda* (11.57) as

माता पुत्रं यथोपस्थे साग्निं बिभर्तु गर्भ आ ।

mātā putraṁ yathopasthe sāgniṁ bibhartu garbha ā

The earth holds the energy in her womb like the mother of her child.

The *Śatapatha Brāhmaṇa* (6.5.1.11) further explains this –

इति यथा माता पुत्रमुपस्थे बिभ्ऽयाद् एवम् अग्निं गर्भे बिभर्त्विति ।

iti yathā mātā putramupasthe bibh'yād evam agniṁ garbhe bibhartviti

Just as a mother carries the child in her womb, similarly earth holds the energy in her womb.

The same fact has been upheld by the *Ś.Br.* (6.5.5.11) and the *Tāṇḍya Brāhmaṇa* (10.1.1). They maintain that this earth is three-layered: energy - hard crust - vegetation. The energy layer is surrounded by the hard crust which is further covered with vegetation. The *Taittirīya Brāhmaṇa* (3.11.1.17) mentions that energy is located in the earth –

अग्निर् असि पृथिव्यां श्रितः ।

agnir asi pṛthivyāṁ śritaḥ

Energy has its shelter in the earth.

At another place (1.1.3.3) the same fact is mentioned in an allegorical manner as –

अग्निर् देवेभ्यो निलायत. आखूरूपं कृत्वा स पृथिवीं प्राविशत् ।

agnir devebhyo nilāyata. ākhūrūpaṁ kṛtvā sa pṛthivīṁ prāviśat.

Energy absconded from luminary bodies and pierced into the earth like a mouse.

The seer of the *Śatapatha Brāhmaṇa* (6.4.1.2) describes geothermal energy as located in the middle of the earth –

पृथिव्या उपस्थाद् अग्निं पशव्यम् ।

pṛthivyā upasthād agniṁ paśavyaṁ

I harness energy that benefits living beings from the middle of the earth.

The above statement points out the harnessing of geothermal energy for various beneficial uses. This harnessing of geothermal energy for various beneficial uses is called Gomedha.

Here, it is also significant to understand that the Nighaṇṭu reads 'gau' among the names of the earth. As such, in the Vedas, the intended meaning of 'gau' is earth. In the Śrauta Sūtras, 'gau' is also intended for earth instead of its apparent meaning ', cow'. Here, it is essential to know that in all the Vedic rituals. However, we find the mention of Puruṣamedha, Aśvamedha, etc., no direct mention of Gomedha is available in them. Yes, we come across a ritual named Gavāmayana, which is a year-long process. This ritual does not mention the sacrifice of a 'cow'. The *Aitareya Brāhmaṇa* (4.17) describes the Gavāmayana ritual. In the opening stanza, it is observed,

गवाम् अयनेन यन्ति । गावो वा आदित्याः । आदित्यानामेव तद् अयनेन यन्ति ।
गावो वै सत्रम् आसत ।

*gavām ayanena yanti. gāvo vā ādityāḥ. ādityānāmeva
tad ayanena yanti. gāvo vai satram āsata.*

[Meaning] Gau is earth, and ayana are movements. Gavāmayana symbolizes the movement of the earth (around the sun). Gaus are verily the rays of the sun. Gavāmayana, therefore, the other way round, represents the tropical movements of the sun or ā ditya on Earth. The Uttarāyaṇa (summer solstice) and Dakṣiṇāyana (winter solstice) are two tropical movements of the sun or Āditya. Thus, Gavāmanayan symbolises Uttarāyaṇa and Dakṣiṇāyana.

It is important to know that Gomedha or Gavālambha symbolizes harnessing the earth's energy for beneficial uses or transmitting it from the centre of the Earth to sterilize the entire global surface, thereby enabling us to inhabit it. Without this geothermal radiation, the earth would have become a desert planet devoid of bio-life.

According to the Vedas, Agni has its abode in the earth. According to the first mantra of the Brahamcharī Sūkta of the *Atharvaveda* (1.5.1) envisaged by Brahma-

ब्रह्मचारीश्चरति रोदसी उभे तस्मिन् देवाः संमनसो भवन्ति ।
स दाधार पृथिवीं दिवं च स आचार्यं तपसा पिपर्ति ॥ अथर्ववेद, 1.5.1

*brahmachārīrścharati rodasī ubhe tasmin devāḥ
saṁmanaso bhavanti,*
*sa dādhāra pṛthivīṁ divaṁ cha sa āchāryaṁ tapasā
piparti.*

(ब्रह्मचारी) A Vedic Scholar (चरति) continuously

focuses (रोदसी) on the Sun and the earth. (देवाः) The parents and teachers (भवन्ति) hold (संमनसो) similar opinions (तस्मिन्) about him. (That is, they are unequivocal about his mission) (सः) He (दाधार) makes judicious use of (दिवम्) solar insolation and (पृथिवीम्) geothermal energy. (सः) He (पिपर्ति) makes the teachings of (आचार्यम्) his teacher successful (तपसा) with his tapas, i.e. new applications of solar and geothermal energies.

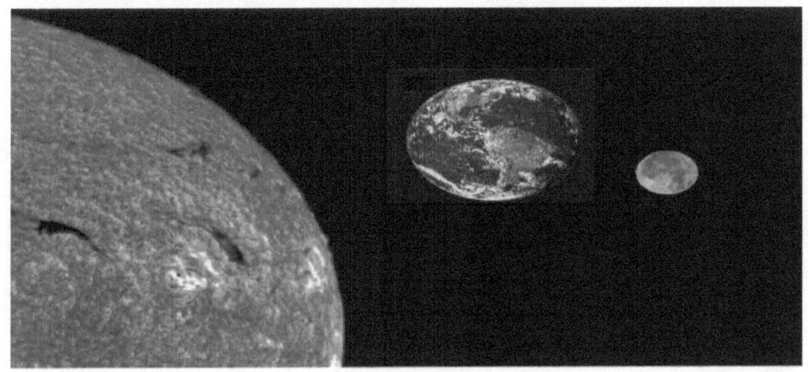

Fig. (Sun and earth)

At another place the Atharvaveda (1.1.10) clearly points out to two sources of energy beneficial to the humanity. The mantra reads as under:

अर्वागन्यः परो अन्यो दिवस्पृष्ठाद् गुहा निधी निहितौ ब्राह्मणस्य ।
तौ रक्षति तपसा ब्रह्मचारी तत् केवलं कृणुते ब्रह्म विद्वान् ॥ अथर्ववेद, 1.1.10

arvāganyaḥ paro anyo divaspṛṣṭhād guhā nidhī nihitau brāhmaṇasya,
tau rakṣati tapasā brahmachārī tat kevalaṁ kṛṇute brahma vidvān.

[Meaning] (निधी) Of the two types of energies (निहितौ) located (गुहा) in the cave (ब्राह्मणस्य) of the universe, (अन्यः) one (अर्वाग्) is very near in the core of earth and (अन्यः) another comes (परः) far away

(दिवः पृष्ठाद्) from the photosphere of the sun. (केवलम्) Only (ब्रह्मचारी) a Vedic scholar (रक्षति) makes good use of (तौ) these two forms of energy (तपसा) with his knowledge. (तत्) This knowledge (कृणुते) makes him a meaningful (ब्रह्म विद्वान्) scholar excelling in the knowledge of the solar system.

Fig. Core of the earth

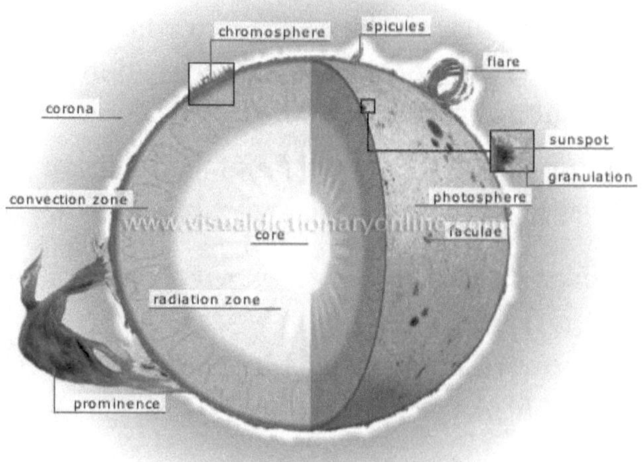

Fig. Photosphere of the sun

In the next mantra (AV. 1.1.11), it is clearly stated that

(अग्री) two sources of Heat Energy (समेतः) are available (इमे) in both of the sun and earth (नभसी अन्तरा) that are mutually bound to each other by the force of attraction. (अन्यः) One (अर्वाक्) is very near (under our feet) and (अन्यः) another (इतः पृथिव्याः) is far away from this earth (in the sun). (रश्मयः) The heat energy emanating (तयोः) from both of these two sources (अधिश्रयन्ते) gets stored in the atmosphere of our planet. (That is to say that crust of the earth, sea surface and winds are jointly heated by the solar insolation and geothermal energy. In other words, the combined effect of both types of energy is responsible for blowing winds, evaporation of waters and from oceans and other water bodies and over all heat content of the earth). (ब्रह्मचारी) The Brahmachārī (Vedic Scholar) (आतिष्ठति) harnesses (तान्) both the energies (तपसा) with his technical knowledge for the benefit of humankind. The mantra reads as follows:

अर्वागन्यः इतो अन्यः पृथिव्याः अग्री समेतो नभसी अन्तरेमे ।
तयोः श्रयन्ते रश्मयो·धि दृढास्तानातिष्ठति तपसा ब्रह्मचारी ॥

arvāganyaḥ ito anyaḥ pṛthivyāḥ agnī sameto nabhasī antareme,
tayoḥ śrayante raśmayo·dhi dṛḍhāstānātiṣṭhati tapasā brahmachārī.

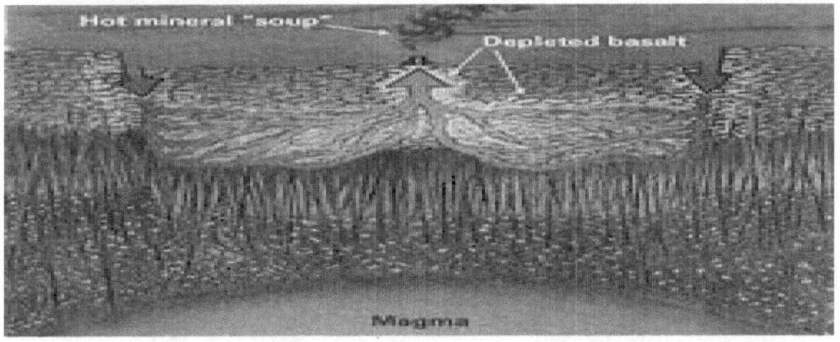

Fig. Geothermal Energy

In addition to the above mantras of the Atharvaveda,

The Rigveda (1.1.1-2) also points out to the fact that geothermal energy is the source of creation on the earth. It was harnessed by the previous seers and new seers are also harnessing it. This fullfills the energy needs of the scholars on this planet.

अग्निमीळे पुरोहितं यज्ञस्य देवं ऋत्विजम् । होतारं रत्नधातमम् ॥

agnimīḻe purohitaṁ yajñasya devaṁ ṛtvijam, hotāraṁ ratnadhātamam.

(ईळे) Let me harness (अग्निम्) the geothermal energy of the earth (पुरोहितम्) that which is the forerunner of (यज्ञस्य) creation on the earth (Note: if a planet is devoid of her geothermal energy she would become a barren planet), (देवम्) that which is highly effulgent, (ऋत्विजम्) that which create things according to their need and time, (होतारम्) that which provides several facilities worth living on the earth and that which (रत्नधातमम्) possesses precious gems available on the earth.

अग्नि पूर्वेभिः ऋषिभिरीड्य नूतनैरूत । स देवां इह वक्षति ॥

agni pūrvebhiḥ ṛṣibhirīḍya nūtanairūta, sa devāṁ iha vakṣati.

(अग्निः) Geothermal energy located in the centre of the earth (ईड्यः) is worthy to be harnessed by both (पूर्वेभिः) ancient (उत) and (नूतनैः) modern (ऋषिभिः) seers/visionary persons. (सः) He (आ वक्षति) sends (देवान्) geothermal radiation (इह) here (on the surface of the earth).

The 12th mantra of the '*Bhūmi Sūkta*' talks about a perennial source of energy in the womb of the earth. It reads as follows:

यत् ते मध्यम् पृथिवी यच्च नाभ्यां यास्त् उर्जः तन्वः सम्भुवुः ।

तासु नो धेह्यभि नः पवस्व माता भुमिः पुत्रो अहं पृथिव्याः ॥

*yat te madhyam pṛthivī yacca nābhyāṁ yāst urjaḥ
tanvaḥ sambhuvuḥ.
tāsu no dhehyabhi naḥ pavasva mātā bhumiḥ putro
ahaṁ prithvyāḥ*

[Meaning] O Earth! In the midst of your body, there is a source of energy, situated exactly at the centre, in your navel. This is your most thematic feature, energizing your entire body. We ought to focus our full attention here only. This is your sanctum sanctorum. The energy transmitted from the centre sterilizes the entire global surface, thereby enabling us to inhabit it. You are vitalizing and sheltering the entire civilization as the mother feeds and looks after her children.

Interestingly, in 1993, American Geophysicist John Marvin Herndon discovered a gigantic self-sustained natural nuclear reactor at the centre of the earth producing four terawatts of heat power output to feed the energy requirement of 1343 active volcanoes, over 10000 hot water springs, movement of lithosphere plates, mid-plate earthquakes, hotspots, tsunamis, mountain building and global heat flow value on the surface of the earth.

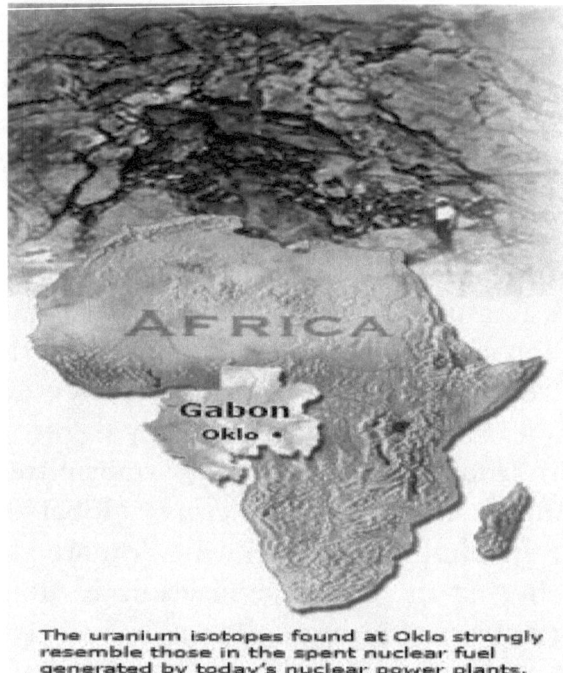

Fig. Natural Nuclear Fission Reactor of the Earth

The radioactive remains of a natural nuclear fission reaction that happened 1.7 billion years ago in Gabon, Africa, were held in place by the surrounding geology.

Thus, the very idea that life on Earth is sustained by the sun alone is wrong. The fact is that the earth is equally responsible for the sustenance of life on it. Planets without their own energy are unable to sustain life even in the presence of the sun. The permutation and combination of solar radiation and geothermal energy generates the atmosphere on earth conducive to sustaining bio-life on the earth.

For earthlings, there are two basic sources of energy: The self-sustained natural nuclear fission reactor operating in the core of the Earth and the self-sustained natural nuclear fusion reactor located in the core of the Sun.

Due to its internally generated energy, the Earth can form its magnetosphere.

The combined effect of solar radiation and geothermal energy drives the atmosphere and oceans into patterns of everyday wind, water, and weather. This allows the earth to maintain an average surface temperature of 15⁰C.

Various Permutations and combinations of geothermal energy and solar radiation are funding the so-called conventional and non-conventional sources of energy, viz., fossil fuels, hydel energy, wind energy, nuclear power reactors, geothermal power plants, solar power plants, and so on.

The role of solar radiation in the growth and development of terrestrial plants (through photosynthesis) and those of marine organisms, including phytoplankton and zooplankton, is noticed by everybody.

The temperature of the caldera of an erupted volcano reaches up to 1200⁰ Centigrade, about 400⁰ Centigrade higher than that of a fossil fuel-fired furnace of an Electric Power Plant. There are 550 active volcanoes and more than 100,000 hot water springs on the earth to provide enough geothermal energy.

Geothermal electricity generation is currently used in 24 countries, while geothermal heating is used in 70 countries. Estimates of the electricity-generating potential of geothermal energy vary from 35 to 2,000 GW. The current worldwide Installed Capacity is 10,715 MW. In recent years, the Indonesian Govt. has announced plans for two 'fast-track' increases in the total capacity of Indonesia's electricity generation network of 10,000 MW each. Geothermal power is considered to be sustainable because the heat extraction is small compared with the earth's heat content. This heat naturally flows to the surface by conduction and is replenished by radioactive decay. The earth's heat content is 10^{31} joules. The estimated electricity-generating potential of geothermal energy can readily provide power at rates, more than double humanity's current energy consumption from primary sources.

The emission intensity of existing geothermal electric plants is on average 122 Kg of CO_2 per megawatt-hour (MW-h) of electricity, about one-eighth of a conventional coal-fired plant. As a result, geothermal power has the potential to help mitigate the global warming if widely deployed in place of fossil fuels. Geothermal has minimal land and freshwater requirements. Geothermal plants use 3.5 square kilometres per gigawatt of electrical production versus 32 square kilometres and 12 square kilometres for coal facilities and wind farms, respectively. They use 20 litres of freshwater per MW-h versus over 1000 litres for nuclear, coal, or oil. Moreover, geothermal power does not rely on variable energy sources, unlike, e.g. wind or solar. Its capacity factor can be pretty significant - up to 96% has been demonstrated. The global average was 73% in 2005.

From the aforementioned, it is very clear that Gomedha is harnessing geothermal energy for beneficial uses and also transmitting it from the centre of the Earth to sterilize the entire global surface, thereby enabling us to inhabit it.

Avi-Medha
The Field Energy
or
The Energy of Intermediate Space

The Avi is described in the Vedas as intermediate space between Chidākāśa (space of Brahman) and Bhūtākāśa (observable space), between stars and their planets or, say, between our sun and earth. In the *Yajurveda* (23.54), Avi is described as pilippilā, which is something very soft that protects and presses very easily. This soft object is nothing but the intermediate space or magnetosphere of the earth having dense field lines. The magnetosphere of Earth protects us from the ultraviolet radiation from the sun. Wool of Avi (sheep) is used to strain soma juice (solar radiation). The intermediate space acts as a strainer of soma juice; the radiation from the sun filters down to Earth through the magnetosphere of the Earth (interface between sun and Earth).

Agni is the first form of energy abiding in light space. The second form of energy is described as 'vāyu', field energy located in the intermediate space or the earth's magnetosphere. The *Taittirīya Upaniṣad* describes the constitution of adhiloka as follows: adhiloka is constituted with the Earth as the first constituent, the Sun as the second constituent, the Antrikṣa (intermediate space) as a link between the two, i.e. earth and sun. Thus, vāyu here is not the 'air' but the Earth's field energy or magnetic field. The 'vāyu' (field lines or field energy) is a link maker between the two, i.e. the Earth and the Sun.

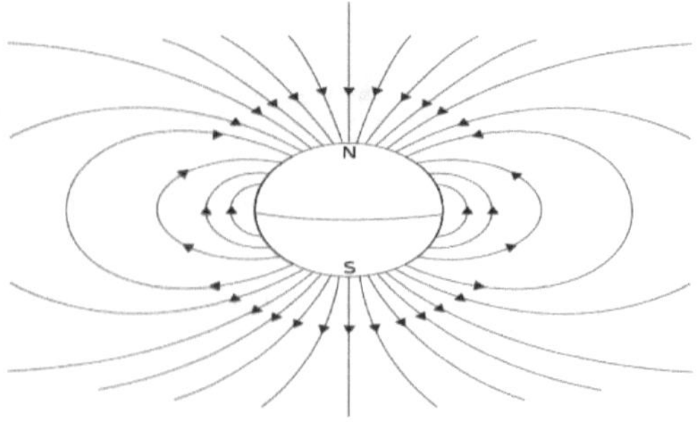

Fig. The magnetic field of the earth

In fact, the earth's magnetic field forms the magnetosphere, which deflects particles from the Solar wind.

The magnetosphere shields the surface of the Earth from the charged particles of the solar wind. The magnetosphere of each heavenly body is generated by the plasma located in the nuclear reactor in their centre (wombs). Similarly, the earth's magnetosphere is generated by plasma, which is located in the nuclear reactor at the centre of the earth. It is compressed on the day (Sun) side due to the force of the arriving particles and extended on the night side.

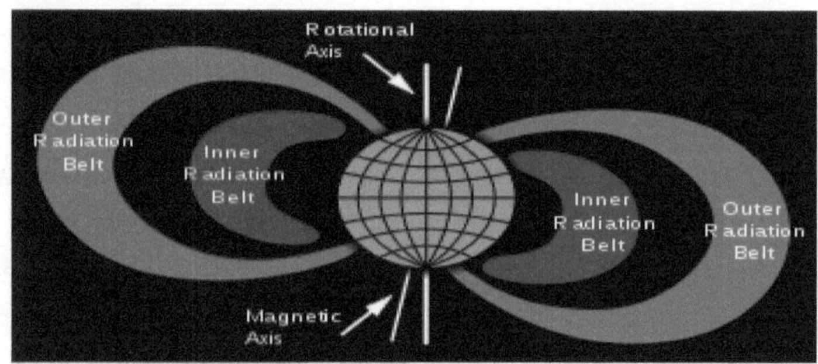

Fig. Radiation belts

The collision between the magnetic field and the

solar wind forms the Radiation belt, a pair of concentric, Torus-shaped regions of energetically charged particles. These radiation belts surrounding the earth are known as Van Allen belts in modern science. Similar radiation belts are also formed around other planets.

Thus if Avi is the intermediate space, Avi medha is the process of collision between the magnetic field and the solar wind forming the Radiation belt. It has been discovered that the Earth's atmosphere limits the belts' particles to regions above 200 - 1,000 kilometres. Here it is significant to understand that until the magnetosphere of the earth was not formed, the earth was a barren planet. Nothing could grow over it. As soon as the Avi (magnetosphere) was formed, the earth became laden with vegetation.

This fact is very beautifully depicted in the *Taittirīya Samhitā* (2.1.2.3) as under:

सा अविर्वशा समभवत् । ते देव अब्रुवन् एवपशुर्वा अयं समभूत् । कस्मा इमम् आलप्स्यामह इति । अथ वै तर्ह्यल्पा पृथिव्यासीत् । अजाता ओषधयः । ताम् अविं वशाम् आदित्येभ्यः कामायालभन्त, ततो वा अप्रथत् पृथिवि, अजायन्त ओषधयः ।

sā avir vaśā samabhavat. te deva abruvan evapaśur vā ayaṁ samabhūt. kasmā imam ālapsyāmaha iti. Atha vai tarhyalpā pṛthvyāsīt. ajātā oṣadhayaḥ. tām aviṁ vaśām ādityebhyaḥ kāmāyālabhanta, tato vāaprayat pṛthivi, ajāyanta oṣadhayaḥ.

[Meaning] Then appeared Avi (the magnetosphere of the earth). The gods proclaimed that this energy field had originated. What should we harness it for? By that time, Earth was a barren planet. No vegetation had grown on it. Avi was harnessed for life on the earth. Thence, the earth became fertile, and vegetation grew on it.

The similar observation is attested in the *Maitrāyaṇī Saṁhitā* as:

अथवा इयं तर्ह्युक्षाऽऽसीद् अलोमिका। ते अब्रुवन् तस्मै कामाय अलभामहै, यथाऽस्याम् ओषध्यश्च वनस्पतयश्च अजायन्त।

athavā iyaṁ tarhyukṣā''sīd alomikā. Te abruvan tasmai kāmāya alabhāmahai, yathā'syām oṣadhyaś ca vanaspatayaś ca ajāyanta.

[Meaning] By that time, the earth was barren without any hair growth (vegetation) over it. Let us desire Avi (the magnetosphere of the earth) so that vegetation may grow on the earth like hairs on the body.

The above observations indicate the essentiality of Avimedha or harnessing Avi energy for the growth of vegetation and life on Earth. In the *Yajurveda* (13.50), Avi is attributed with the epithet of *ūrṇāyu* (woollen cover) and described as a protective skin cover of *paśus* (*tvacaṁ paśūnām*)-

इमम् ऊर्णायुं वरुणस्य नाभिं त्वचं पशूनाम्।

imam ūrṇāyuṁ varuṇasya nābhiṁ tvacaṁ paśūnām.

It may also be noted that field lines of intermediate space act as a woollen filter for solar radiation to reach the Earth. These field lines, in fact, act as the skin cover of the earth to shield it from solar winds. That is why Avi is attributed with the above epithets.

Ajā-Medha

Active Energy not yet converted into Matter

In the *Śatapatha Brāhmaṇa* (6.5.1.4), aja or ajā (vikṛti/active energy) is described as the form of all animals (matter particles). It signifies ajā as the active energy of the Bhūtākāśa (observable space). Unborn energy is energy that has not been converted into matter particles. For this universe to get going, energy has to convert into matter. It is the form of all other animals (matter particles), like Aśva (solar energy), Gau (geothermal energy) and Avi (field energy or energy located in the magnetosphere). Aja in the *Atharvaveda* (9.5.7) is considered agni (active energy).

अजो अग्निः (*ajo agniḥ*)

The *Atharvaveda* (9.5.13) further says that Aja (active energy) was born from the perturbation or agitation of Agni (inactive energy) by the Saṅkalpa of Brahman.

अजो ह्यश्ग्नेरजनिष्ट शोकाद्

ajo hyalgnerajaniṣṭa śokād

The *Yajurveda* (13.51) and the *Atharvaveda* (4.14.1) also maintain that Ajā was born from the perturbation/agitation (śoka) of agni (inactive energy) and he saw agni (active energy) first and gods (matter particles) became gods (matter particles) due to Aja (activation of energy).

अजो ह्यग्नेरजनिष्ट शोकात्सो अपश्यज्जनितारमग्रे ।
तेन देवा देवतामग्रयँस्तेन रोहमायन्नुप मेध्यासः ।। यजु. 13.51

ajo hyagnerajaniṣṭa śokātso apaśyajjanitāramagre.

tena devā devatāmagrayaṁstena rohamāyannupa

medhyāsaḥ. Yaj. S. 13.51

अजो ह्यश्ग्रेरजनिष्ट शोकात्सो अपश्यज्जनितारमग्रे ।
तेन देवा देवतामग्र आयन्तेन रोहन्नुरुहुर्मेध्यासः ।। अथर्ववेद 4.14.1

ajo hya?gnerajaniṣṭa śokātso apaśyajjanitāramagre;
tena devā devatāmagra āyantena
rohanruruhurmedhyāsaḥ.

Atharvaveda 4.14.1

Similar observations have been held in the *Śatapatha Brāhmaṇa* (6.5.4.13), wherein it is mentioned that ajā (active energy of the bhūtākāśa is the result of the śoka (saṅkalpa) of Prajāpati (Brahman).

प्रजापतेर्वै शोकादजा समभवन् ।

prajāpatervai śokādajā samabhavan.

At another place in the *Śatapatha Brāhmaṇa* (14.1.2.13), it has been mentioned that ajā is the result of the tapa (saṅkalpa) of the Prajāpati, so it is called the sibling born of tapa.

तपसो ह वाऽएषा प्रजापतेः सम्भूता यदजा तस्मादाह तपसस्तनूरसीति ।

tapaso ha vā'eṣā prajāpateḥ sambhūtā yadajā tasmādāha tapasastanūrasīti.

This all points out that active energy (vikṛti) is this visible world's material source of origin. Aja (unborn active energy) is described in the *Ṛgveda* (7.35.13) as having one foot (ekapāda).

शं नो अज एकपादेवो अस्तु

śaṁ no aja ēkapāddevo astu

[Meaning] Let this one-fourth active energy of the Bhūtākāśa (observable space) be favourable to us.

Similarly, the *Śatapatha Brāhmaṇa* (8.2.4.1) mentions that one fourth part of ajā of Chidākāśa became active in Bhūtākāśa.

एकपदा ह भूत्वाऽजा उच्चक्रमुः ।

ēkapadā ha bhūtvā'jā uchchakramuḥ

[Meaning] One-fourth part of ajā (prakṛti or inactive energy) became active in Bhūtākāśa.

This shows that out of the total inactive energy of Chidākāśa, only 25% is active in Bhūtākāśa. The ajā is compared to a night in the *Yajurveda* (23.54). It is also described as piśiṅgilā, meaning devourer of visible matter. The visible universe is born of active energy and again consumed into it. Ajā is piśiṅgilā, which devours universal objects during dissolution. Ajā (active energy) also means unborn until it does not convert into matter particles; sometimes it is called once born (ekaja) because, in one creation cycle, it is activated once and not again and again.

द्यौरासीत्पूर्वचित्तिरश्व आसीद् बृहद्वयः ।
अविरासीत्पिलिप्पिला रात्रिरासीत्पिशिङ्गिला ।। यजु. 23.55

dyaurāsītpūrvachittiraśva āsīd bṛhadvayaḥ ।
avirāsītpilippilā rātrirāsītpiśiṅgilā ।। Yaj. 23.55

[Meaning] Chidākāśa (space of Brahman) is the first storehouse of energy. Aśva (stars/sun) is the biggest source of energy in the Bhūtāśa (observable space). Avi (intermediate space or magnetosphere) is the protector and ajā (active energy in Bhūtākāśa) is the devourer of this material world during dissolution.

Thus, Aja or Ajā is active energy, and Ajāmedha is

nothing else but the process of converting active energy into matter particles and material objects.

Here, it may be pointed out that in Agnihotra, there is a provision for ājyāhutis. Ājyāhutis are offered with ghee. The ājyāhutis symbolize the ahuti of ajā (active energy) in the yajña of creation. Matter is formed when āhuti of ajā (active energy) is offered in the yajña of creation. Ghee also symbolizes (active energy).

9 789394 724099